Praise for

WOVE

"The compassionate, experienced guide we needed all along as we reimagine faith formation with generosity and love."

—Sarah Bessey, *New York Times* bestselling author of
A Rhythm of Prayer and *Jesus Feminist*

"A clear and kind guide for those of us attempting to disentangle our faith while raising kids in that faith. Meredith helps parents hand down a faith not based on obedience to a checklist, but trust in a God who desires a relationship. If you are searching for a way forward after deconstruction or disenchantment, there is no better co-pilot than this book, and truthfully, anything Meredith puts out into the world."   —Erin Moon, co-host of *The Bible Binge* podcast

"Parenting is difficult and beautiful, and adding faith to the mix just makes it more of both. When I started reading *Woven*, I wept with relief. Literal tears. I didn't realize the desert I was in until Meredith Miller offered me water. This book is an absolute gift, and I will now aggressively press it into as many hands as possible."

—Kendra Adachi, *New York Times* bestselling author of
The Lazy Genius Way and *The Lazy Genius Kitchen*

"*Woven* is for every parent who feels overwhelmed and undertrained—meaning all of us. Based on her stellar research and real-life experience, Meredith Miller offers parents a winning combination for family faith formation: Biblical wisdom translated into everyday ideas that you and I can try at home."

—Kara Powell, PhD, Chief of Leadership Formation at
Fuller Seminary and co-author of *3 Big Questions*
That Change Your Teenager

"*Woven* took my shriveled, prune-like confidence in raising my kids within a healthy Christian framework and nurtured it into a big, fat, juicy confidence plum. If you are someone who is actively re-learning and re-engaging their faith alongside their children, Meredith's words will give you the tools and courage to have challenging, faith-based conversations with your kids, even when you yourself don't have all the answers."

—Kelly Bandas, author of *Rookie Mistakes:*
A Grown-Up's Field Guide for Getting Your Act Together

"At last, an alternative to confusion and fear. *Woven* is the new classic we've been waiting for. Meredith Miller gives us practical tools, presents a clear path forward, and reminds us it's never too late to change course. I want to put this book in the hands of every Jesus-loving parent I know."

—Shannan Martin, author of *Start with Hello* and
The Ministry of Ordinary Places

"I've never read a Christian parenting book quite like *Woven*—and I'm so grateful to have it now. *Woven* is a guiding light for our times and our real lives…. *Woven* helps us untangle Christ from culture and reminds us who God is—and how that can inform how we nurture and care for the faith lives of our families. I highlighted and underlined my way through this thoughtful, theological, and highly accessible book."

—Kayla Craig, author of *Every Season Sacred* and
To Light Their Way; creator of Liturgies
for Parents on Instagram

WOVEN

WOVEN

NURTURING A FAITH YOUR KID
DOESN'T HAVE TO HEAL FROM

MEREDITH MILLER

New York • Nashville

Worthy
Hachette Book Group
1290 Avenue of the Americas, New York, NY 10104
worthypublishing.com
@WorthyPub

Originally published in hardcover and ebook by Worthy in August 2023
First trade paperback edition: August 2024

Worthy is a division of Hachette Book Group, Inc. The Worthy name and logo are registered trademarks of Hachette Book Group, Inc.

The publisher is not responsible for websites (or their content) that are not owned by the publisher.

The Hachette Speakers Bureau provides a wide range of authors for speaking events. To find out more, go to hachettespeakersbureau.com or email HachetteSpeakers@hbgusa.com.

Worthy Books may be purchased in bulk for business, educational, or promotional use. For information, please contact your local bookseller or the Hachette Book Group Special Markets Department at special.markets@hbgusa.com.

Scripture quotations noted NASB are from the NEW AMERICAN STANDARD BIBLE. Copyright © 1960, 1962, 1963, 1968, 1971, 1972, 1973, 1975, 1977, 1995 by The Lockman Foundation. Used by permission. All rights reserved. http://www.lockman.org.

Scripture quotations noted NIV are taken from the Holy Bible, New International Version®. Copyright © 1973, 1978, 1984, 2011 by Biblica, Inc.™ Used by permission of Zondervan. All rights reserved worldwide. www.zondervan.com. The "NIV" and "New International Version" are trademarks registered in the United States Patent and Trademark Office by Biblica, Inc.™

Scripture quotations noted NLT are from the *Holy Bible*, New Living Translation, copyright © 1996, 2004, 2015 by Tyndale House Foundation. Used by permission of Tyndale House Publishers, Inc., Carol Stream, Illinois 60188. All rights reserved.

Print book interior design by Bart Dawson.

Library of Congress Control Number: 2023003970

ISBNs: 978-1-5460-0436-3 (trade paperback), 978-1-5460-0437-0 (ebook)

Printed in the United States of America

LSC-C

Printing 2, 2024

To Curtis, Riley, and Peyton

CONTENTS

Introduction xi

PART I

Chapter 1: Walls and Webs 3

Chapter 2: Weave Your Own Web 21

Chapter 3: Do Less On Purpose 45

Chapter 4: About the Bible 63

PART II

Chapter 5: God Is Good 89

Chapter 6: God Is Powerful 113

Chapter 7: God Is Just 133

Chapter 8: God Is Joyful 155

Chapter 9: God Is With Us 173

Chapter 10: Jesus Is Lord 191

Chapter 11: Where Webs Begin 215

Acknowledgments 231

About the Author 233

INTRODUCTION

Let's be clear about one thing from the beginning of this book: I hate spiders. Like, "thought about choosing a different guiding metaphor for this book" hate them. I hate the ratio of body to leg, and how finding one is the worst kind of surprise.

Paradoxically, I also hate killing spiders. The anthropomorphic part of me kicks in and I imagine that the spider is all scared and confused to be in my house, surrounded by giant, stomping humans, and I can't bear to smoosh it. So I don't. I try to save it, scooping it up on a spare piece of paper, or trapping it in a handy cup and making for the nearest exit. One summer I worked for a camp and slept in a tent in the woods. Spiders entered our tent on the regular, and I still did not kill a single one, not even for the sake of a group of kids.

Every time I find myself separated from those tiny, creeping legs by nothing but a piece of junk mail, rushing to the door, I think, *What in the world am I doing?*

Whatever it is I'm doing, my kids seem to be catching on, at least a bit, because they now *insist* that I save the spiders who find their way into our home. So now I'm stuck. As much as my insides might be flip-flopping as the little legs scramble toward my hand, the fact of the matter is I *want* to save the spiders for my kids. With any luck, my Great and Noble Sacrifice will help my kids learn a bit of what it means to care for what God has made, big and small.

Parenting is full of these "I want to do this for my kids but wow does it make me uncomfortable" sorts of situations, some of which are far bigger deals than spider rescue missions. Perhaps you feel a similar discomfort when it comes to introducing your kids to God. You want to. It matters to you. But talking about the Bible (why, oh why, are the stories so confusing?); or praying out loud (why is my word-maker suddenly not forming the sounds?); or any number of other things you think "good Christian parents" do leave you thinking, *What in the world am I doing?*

Here's the bad news (for me and any other spider-haters reading this): We are going to need to talk about spiders—or at least their webs—a fair bit more. Here's the good news: A spider's web may just be the very image that helps us embrace the discomfort and find our way forward in the important work of becoming a family that follows Jesus together. Fascinating things, webs, but more on that in the next chapter. First, let's unpack that discomfort of introducing our kids to God a bit more.

"Miss Charlotte, we don't do that in the four-year-old room," I piped up from my spot on the sea of blue industrial carpet. The four-year-old room at church was my happy place, because we had a rocking boat toy that transformed into stairs when flipped upside down, and the snack was Goldfish crackers, which we didn't keep at home.

Charlotte Greenacre was faithfully present and unwaveringly gentle, with a voice so soft you wanted to snuggle into it for a nice, warm nap. She was a grandmother not only to her own family, but to our church family, especially my Sunday school class.

But when she went to lead prayer that day, she did it wrong. I don't remember why. But I do know I told her so.

Apparently, I have always been opinionated about how to help kids meet God. (My parents may tell you I've always been opinionated about darn near everything else, too, but I digress.)

I suspect you might also have opinions about how *your* child meets God, and that those opinions have gotten a tad more complicated as your own journey of faith has moved well past the "eating Goldfish crackers in the four-year-old room" stage. Maybe your journey has included enough pain, uncertainty, and confusion that you're not always sure who this God is that you want your child to meet. And, can this God even be trusted in the first place?

Perhaps you feel like God can be trusted, but the Bible is suspect, given how it's been weaponized and how confusing it can be. Or maybe you're good with the Jesus you find in the Bible, but it's the church that's unsafe, given how it has hurt you.

Maybe, after all you've been through trying to follow Jesus, you're wondering how you can introduce your child to a faith they won't have to heal from.

Parenting in real time while simultaneously working out how *you* want to follow Jesus can feel like riding in an airplane that's just hit extreme turbulence. Disoriented and jostled, you need life-giving oxygen. Only instead of a pair of masks dropping—one for you and one for your child—there are dozens to choose from, and while many deliver clean air, you know that at least some carry toxic gas. You also know you're supposed to put your own mask on first, but which one should you grab? And which one will give your child the clean air they need?

- I want to talk about the Bible with my kids.
- Let's hold off on the Bible—it's too confusing and age-inappropriate.
- I want my kid to attend church.
- I'm just not sure I can trust what a church is going to say to my kid.
- I want to pray with my child.
- It seems like prayer just sets them up to be disappointed when God doesn't appear to answer.

Perhaps you've already weathered the turbulence of your own changing and growing faith, and things are smooth again, though the view out the window attests that you're in a new place. You may still feel a desire to help in your own child's journey but also confusion about how to do so. If nothing else, it may be that you're hoping to spare them from some of what you had to go through yourself.

Whether your faith feels stable or jostled, helping your child grow in knowing Jesus can feel challenging. With so many theological positions, and biblical interpretations, and church traditions to choose from, which way is most life-giving for you and for your child? What about your questions? Should you simply wait until you have answers of your own, and then pass those on? But what if that waiting for answers keeps going and going while your kid keeps growing and growing?

Two of my most dearly held opinions (which, as we've established already, is really saying something) are that the God of the Bible is a life-giving God, and that the Jesus we meet in Scripture can be trusted. I suspect you're reading this because you agree, or at least want to agree, and because of that you wonder if you might introduce your child to Jesus now, before you feel completely ready.

So let me say these things up front: There *is* a way for you to introduce your kid to God, even when the God *you* were told about as a kid doesn't totally align with who you believe God to be now. You can still talk about the Bible now that you know how mysterious and unwieldy a book it really is. You can offer answers to your child's questions about faith even when you now have so many questions of your own. This book will help you learn how.

As I grew up, Miss Charlotte told me about that Sunday morning many times, always with amusement in her eyes. She was one of many adults who introduced me to a Jesus I could trust. As a parent and a pastor, I'm trying to do the same, and a spiderweb is helping me know how.

WHERE WE'RE GOING

This book is divided into two parts. Part 1 (chapters 1–4) lays out a variety of factors that contribute to how we nurture healthy faith for our kids. Chapter 1 shares *why* a spiderweb is our guiding image and explains the trust-based paradigm that informs the entire book. Chapter 2 will talk about unhelpful approaches to avoid and needed components to include, even as we expect to create something unique to our family. Chapter 3 will lay out a strategy for faith content. From Bible stories to doctrinal statements, how do we approach the information a child needs? Chapter 4 is devoted entirely to how to introduce the Bible with children.

Since our hope is to help our kids get to know who God is, part 2 (chapters 5–11) will focus on six attributes of God that anchor a strong but adaptable faith. We'll answer the question: How might we help our children anchor themselves to the God who is [each attribute]? Each of the six attributes helps kids of any age to know who God is and to understand the story of the Bible. Even better, they can expand, deepen, and be added to as your child grows.

Maybe most importantly, I've included both reflection prompts and right-now ideas to help your family be able to actually weave that sort of a faith in your real lives, which I'd encourage you to explore as you go so that when you get to the final chapter you'll be able to bring it all together. Chapter 11 will guide you through a process of deciding what comes next for you and your family that can serve you long after you're finished with these pages.

WOVEN

PART I

CHAPTER 1

Walls and Webs

In 2007, I sat down for a coffee I didn't know would completely change the way I thought about my vocation. At a hightop table brightly lit by the sun pouring in through the window of our seminary's bookstore/coffee shop, I met Brad Griffin. Brad is now a senior director at the Fuller Youth Institute (FYI), a preeminent research group housed at Fuller Theological Seminary that studies the faith development of teens. At the time, though, Brad was one of just three on staff at FYI, which had recently launched one of its first research undertakings, then called the College Transition Project. The name was later changed to Sticky Faith, which, you have to admit, was a good call. I asked if I could help as a research assistant, and Brad said yes. I'd never been a research assistant before, and it took me a while to learn how to actually be helpful to the project. It's probably a good thing that I didn't need to be paid.

Fast-forward a bit to when a small group of us were gathered around a gray conference table in a gray room with gray carpet, reviewing printouts of coded data from the study. By now I'd met the faculty members from the School of Psychology who were also part of the research team, and the doctoral students they had invited to be research assistants as well. It turned out that doctoral students in psychology, unlike yours truly, *did* know how to be helpful. And apparently, since this room was in their section of the school, they knew color was *un*helpful.

The data we were reviewing related to how the young people in the study, who were a diverse-in-as-many-ways-as-possible contingent of youth group graduates from around the United States, described their faith across the transition out of high school. One word captured the theme: *moralistic.*

And we were not surprised.

Moralism, simply put, is the idea that the purpose of religion is to create moral humans. You know, good people. Being moral, upstanding, and virtuous is the aim, and religion is a tool to accomplish it. How does religion do that? First, by naming and reinforcing the value of being moral; and second, by communicating that the deity of that religion is pleased by your morality and displeased by your lack of it. It says, "You make God sad when you don't pick up your toys."

When I say these young people described their faith in ways that were moralistic, I mean that they believed God cared most of all about how they acted. They knew the "rules," all the things they should and should not do. Keep your clothes on. Bring your friends to youth group. Don't do drugs. Modify swear words into not-quite swear words. That sort of thing. They had those lists down pat. But more than that, they understood that these lists showed what a good *Christian* should and should not do. Being a good Christian *meant* being a good person. In other words, list management was the main practice of their faith, because the lists made them moral, right, and good Christians. And that made God happy with them.

I want to be as clear as I can: The issue is not the desire for our children to follow God in practical action and attitude. Nor is it a hope that we can guide them to wise choices and away from foolish ones, thereby sparing them some difficult experiences.

The issue is when adults tell kids exactly what fruit should look like in their lives instead of helping them get to know the Spirit who grows the fruit. It's when we fail to recognize that fruit can be faked by a kid, especially if they fear the disapproval of a loved one. Fruit cannot grow in the soil of fear. That is true if the fear belongs to a child who wants us to affirm them, and it's true if the fear belongs to an adult who can't handle the long, slow, out-of-their-control process of helping children discover for themselves who God is. The issue is when we care more about the artificial fruit of compliance, or respect, or first-time listening, than the genuine, juicy fruit of coming alive to the love of the true God and the chance to share that love with the world.

In 2009, a landmark sociological study of religion and faith in American teenagers was published as the book *Soul Searching*.[1] One of the key findings was that the faith of many Americans (it actually goes beyond just teens) can be summarized with a three-word term:

---

[1] Christian Smith, *Soul Searching: The Religious and Spiritual Lives of American Teenagers* (Oxford: Oxford University Press, 2005).

"moralistic therapeutic deism" (MTD). When teens described their religious faith and practice in their own words, these three themes kept popping up. Their faith was moralistic—religion is about being a good person. It was therapeutic—religion is meant to make me feel better. And it was deistic—god is basically far away, but might make an appearance now and then when I need help. It is, in the words of Pastor Al Han, "be good, feel good religion." Notably, MTD was not unique to a single religious tradition, but spanned nearly every group included in the study.

When *Soul Searching* was released, ministry practitioners were abuzz. The consensus was that this articulated what so many of us experienced in our local faith communities. How can we help young people move away from moralistic therapeutic deism? This was the problem to solve!

Unfortunately, little has changed in the decade or so since MTD was first named, perhaps because it was seen as a threat from the outside instead of a flaw on the inside. Church curriculum and family resources alike continued with models that elevated obedient behavior, raising kids in ways that were aligned with, not distinct from, this framing. In fact, the influence of certain brand-name pastors, who are loud on social media, has created the impression for some that an obedience-centric approach to faith is the *only* biblical model, and that since obedience is right, a parent needs to focus on it most of all.

That day around the conference table, as we were puzzling over the factors that had resulted in these young people's faith collapsing into list management, I realized something. See, I was the person in the group whose background was in children's, rather than youth, ministry. I'd been involved in teaching, writing lessons for, and designing programs to serve kids and families for almost ten years by then. What I realized was this: If the faith of teens was mainly moralistic, that hadn't started in youth group. It had started in Sunday school.

THE PROBLEM WITH RAISING "GOOD KIDS"

From ages two through twelve, roughly, most kids who attend church are told Bible stories and play Bible games and eat Bible snacks and make Bible crafts. Each week they are taught exactly what to do to obey God. These messages are echoed at home as well. And maybe also at school.

"Well, what's wrong with that?" a Christian parent may ask. "Obedience is taught all throughout the Bible. God wants people to obey."

This is a fundamental question: Is obedient behavior what God most wants from, and for, children?

"Of course," this Christian parent continues, "Jesus' final commission to the disciples was '[Teach] them to obey everything I have commanded you.'"[2] But *what* Jesus commanded them regarding kids was "Let the little children come to me, and do not hinder them..."[3]

Jesus wanted children to be able to come to him. Not to follow his rules, but to know him.

What's more, if we turn to the Bible's treatment of obedience, what we find is that the obedience God invites people into, both then and now, is a response to trusting God. Again and again in the

---

[2] Matt. 28:20 NIV
[3] Matt. 19:14 NIV

Bible, Yahweh God goes first, acting with power and love on the people's behalf. God calls Abram, frees the Hebrews from enslavement in Egypt, sends manna and water in the wilderness. God becomes a human like us in Jesus, who goes first as he stops beneath Zacchaeus's tree, goes first in speaking to the woman at the well, goes first in offering his body and blood at the table and then in reality.

These actions reveal to God's people what *this* God is like (as compared to the many other deity options called by many other names). As God goes first, they grow in knowing, loving, and trusting Yahweh God. As they find this God to be trustworthy, they change their actions. Did you know the very word translated as "faith" in English refers not to what one believes in their mind, but whom one trusts, in the ultimate sense? The story of Scripture revolves around this trust, often by making a case that God is trustworthy, and the gods of the nations are untrustworthy.

Trust is always the precursor to obedience. The people's obedience is not the first course of action they take, but rather a responsive action based on their determination that yes, indeed, Yahweh God of Israel can be trusted.

Yes, obedience is talked about a lot in the Bible, but obedience is not our goal, because, ultimately, it is not God's goal.

Trust is.

The Ten Commandments offer one helpful example. Often viewed as a list of dos and don'ts, a guide to being obedient, they cannot be separated from the larger story of God freeing the Hebrews from slavery, leading them to safety, and promising them a future. The Ten Commandments are found in Exodus 20, with the reminder of how they continue the exodus story and of who this God is who has saved them and is now making them a community: "I am [Yahweh] your God, who rescued you from the land of Egypt, the place of your slavery."[4] What's more, when we rewind the story a bit, we first see this in Exodus 14:31: "When the Israelites saw the mighty hand of [Yahweh] displayed against the Egyptians, the people feared [Yahweh] and put their trust in [Them[5]] and in Moses [Their] servant" (NIV).

But trust only happens, for kids and adults alike, when we can come to Jesus. We all need the opportunity to explore whether or not God can be trusted. Just like the people from the world of the Bible, we need to discover what *this* God is like, because just like those people, we have many other deity options, both in terms of formal religions and less formal ones, like money, power, or status. And just like them, as we find this God to be trustworthy, we change our actions. Trust changes us. It shapes our identity, our way of being in the world. If healthy obedience ever happens, it's because it's animated by trust.

When it comes to our kids, we have to be clear: It's backward to ask a child to obey a God they do not know. Childhood is for getting to know God, so kids can discover if God can be trusted.

When we bump obedience to the number one spot over trust, we deny children the chance to experience the same process that God's people were offered. Instead of a process, they get lists. Even if the actions included on the dos and don'ts lists are precisely the things God wants for us, by dictating them *to* children, we have set them up for a moralistic faith that says what God cares about most

---

[4] v. 2 NLT

[5] When I'm speaking of God, I sometimes use the singular *They* and *Them*, which I'll note by capitalizing it. If I'm speaking of Jesus, I use *he* and *him*. I find the singular *They* can be one helpful way to (a) use language that reflects the fact that God is not male; and (b) remind me that God is more expansive than and distinct from human beings.

is that they follow the rules and be good kids. We end up using the Bible as if it were a morality-producing manual, instead of the story that reveals who God is. What often gets called obedience is actually moralism, teaching kids to *be* good rather than helping them get to know the God who *is* good.

PARENTING FROM
A TRUST-BASED PARADIGM

This book operates from a trust-based paradigm, rather than an obedience-training one. In a trust-based paradigm, my goal as a parent when it comes to faith is to offer my child time, space, and experiences to help them get to know who God really is. My hope is for my child to discover that because of who God is, God can be trusted. I'd love for you to consider what it would be like to nurture your child's faith from a trust-based paradigm as well. For many reasons, this could be challenging: if you're still wondering yourself if God can be trusted or if you've been hammered so hard by obedience-is-everything that the trust-centered model feels precarious, for instance. But shifting to a trust-based paradigm, seen through the long view, is the first step in nurturing a faith your child won't need to heal from.

On the wall of my kitchen are two framed quotes from Julia Child: "Fat gives things flavor"; and "If you're afraid of butter, use cream." Butter is amazing. Yet, more times than I'd like, I flat-out forget to add it to our Friday pancakes (a ritual in our home). Sometimes I never even get it out of the fridge. Other times I melt it in the microwave and leave it there. Leaving things in the microwave is something of a theme in my life. More often than I care to admit my coffee sits in there so long that I just have to re-re-heat it when I finally look around and wonder where my mug is and realize it's been in the microwave all this time.

But back to pancakes. Let me tell you: Butter-less pancakes are inferior to pancakes with butter. Butter may be simple, not top-of-mind when you think *pancake*, perhaps. But it is an essential ingredient.

As with pancakes and any other culinary creation worth making, parenting from a trust-based paradigm depends upon a simple, unflashy, but nonetheless essential ingredient: taking the long view. Whatever short-term choices we might make come from the long view. In the long run, I want to help kids know and follow God for a lifetime. I hope they come to value life in a local faith community. I want them to experience being known and loved and part of the people of God. I hope they understand their own spiritual gifts and offer them for the good of the world. I hope they trust Jesus wholly.

Though I wish it were different, the truth is much of what happens in the long run is outside of my control. My child is their own person, and their relationship with God is, and always will be, their own. But even though I know this, I'll still admit I have at times been a bit too confident that if I do it all just right, I can do over the course of my kid's childhood years what is actually the Holy Spirit's work to do over a lifetime.

What is mine to do, though, is to intentionally craft short-term strategies that support my child in their faith journey. Ultimately, this entire book is devoted to helping you determine what those strategies will be for your child and your family.

WALLS AND WEBS

Once we've settled on the goal of helping our kids discover that God can be trusted based on who God is, we then face a new challenge: The fact that who God is, is not simple. Sometimes we act as if God is, or should be, simple, but it shouldn't be surprising that God is at least as complex as human beings are. Since *we're* a bundle of seeming contradictions, competing priorities, and conflicting desires, we ought to expect God to be similarly intricate.

But it never fails to catch us by surprise when the God we thought we had a handle on doesn't seem to match up with the God we see in Scripture, or that others talk about, or that a pastor describes. When confronted with this sort of disorientation, there's a natural temptation to respond by latching on to and overemphasizing certain attributes of God (the ones we like best, of course), which inevitably leaves us with an incomplete, even unhelpful understanding of God and ourselves.

As much as we might wish it were different, there's no getting to know God without confronting tension.

God is mystery. And yet, God comes near to us and makes Themself known through the Bible, through Jesus, in nature. Both are true. God is mystery. God is knowable.

The Bible is full of these seeming contradictions and competing themes; all true, but impossible to hold in one simple picture. Our brains want to simplify, to make things understandable. So we hold on to one side and push the other away, only to end up with distortion, which leads to confusion when we are confronted with the reality of a fuller picture of God.

God is love, we say; that's what's true. So...what is all this violence about?

God is justice, we say. So…why don't bad people get what they deserve?

And this tension brings us, of course, to philosophy (bear with me for just one minute; I promise it'll be helpful).

Let's talk about a branch of philosophy called epistemology. Or, in words actual humans use: the question of how knowledge works. How do we know what things are true? There was a long era (dates for this sort of thing get fuzzy, so let's say roughly from the 1600s to the 1900s) when philosophers looked around, presumably at a cathedral or something, and said, "Aha, knowledge is like that!"

In modern philosophy (what this era is often called), knowledge is like a wall. I lay a sturdy foundation of knowledge and facts, and then I can build on top of that layer with another layer of knowledge, and then another. Each layer follows from and rests upon the layer before.

If we've thought that faith, too, is like a wall, and that the purpose of childhood is to "give kids a firm foundation," it's due in large part to the way modernity has influenced our understanding of knowledge.

But somewhere in the 1900s (again, the dates are fuzzy), postmodern philosophers came along asking whether another image might better describe the way our minds, and the world, actually work. Maybe knowledge is more like a web.

In a web, the things we know are like the strands, all interconnected, rather than being built on top of one another. There are still anchor points that hold the web in place, but the structure is flexible, pliable, able to endure stress and even certain amounts of breakage while still surviving.

Did you make it through? Excellent! Let's turn to faith, then.

Here's the key question: Is our faith more wall or web? As a parent, am I helping my child build a wall, or weave a web?

If my faith is a wall, then I begin by selecting foundation stones, key doctrinal statements, perhaps, or traits of God upon which I build my beliefs. And then I build another layer of beliefs on top of the foundational beliefs, and then another layer on top of that one. But then, because this is the not-at-all-simple God we're talking about here, one of those beliefs gets exposed as not being true, or one of those competing themes that are all through the Bible appears. Even something as good and true as "God is love," if it is seen as a foundation stone for a wall, built brick by brick, will have to confront other true attributes of God—like justice.

What now?

If my faith is a wall, there are two options: I can explain away the new information that doesn't fit in the wall I've built, or I can take out a stone. The wall will hold for a while, with holes here and there. But what happens to a wall when too many stones get removed? The whole thing topples over. In other words, I can either ignore reality or see my reality crumble to the ground.

The problem with seeing our faith as a wall is that when one of the stones gets exposed as not being true, or not being true in the way we thought it was, we think we need to tear the whole thing down and start over again. Worse, unless we're *really* good at ignoring reality, the wall falls whether we want to tear it down or not. We find ourselves standing amid the rubble of our former faith, wondering how we will ever rebuild.

Perhaps we can summon the energy to search for better foundation stones. Perhaps the destruction is too great to even imagine rebuilding.

But what if our faith, like other kinds of knowing, is not a wall? What if our faith is a web?

"And then there's funnel webs, and tangle webs, and sheet webs, and orb webs. And…"

Our younger son hadn't even clambered up into his car seat yet and he was in full flow. He had learned about spider webs at pre-school that day, and so now, as is always the case when he learns something new, every precious drop of information was rushing out in a torrent of words. Who knew there was so much to say about spiders' webs?

As I learned that day, webs can take on an astounding variety of shapes, while still sharing some common features: anchor strands that hold the web in place, internal strands that give it shape and texture and beautiful complexity. I trust you have, at some point in your life, looked closely at a spider's web. It's fascinatingly intricate, seemingly so fragile, and yet it's a spider's home, its source of nourishment, its protection. A web is a spider's way of adapting to the endlessly complex, maddeningly unpredictable, frighteningly unstable world in which it lives. And that's what makes it such a helpful image for our faith.

A web anchors itself at many points, with strong strands that provide its basic structure. Each anchor thread is upheld by tension and expects to be stretched. Meanwhile, the internal strands make up the body of the web so that it has its own unique shape, texture, complexity, beauty. Anchor threads and internal threads combine to create something incredibly resilient. You may not have known, but spiders' webs are considered incredibly strong, not because they rigidly withstand the elements, but because they can bend without breaking in the face of them.

Perhaps our faith works in a similar fashion. Anchor threads affix to who God is, including the attributes that live in mysterious, dynamic tension with one another. Internal threads—habits; less essential, but still important beliefs; faith practices; life rhythms—give our faith its unique shape.

Then there's what happens when breakage does occur. A web is designed with the *expectation* that strands will break, and with resources for repair. When the web does break, it's not because the spider failed; the web was made for this. Unlike a wall, which topples over if too much wind comes along, webs are designed so that if the wind blows extra hard, or a stick falls through it, a few of the strands will break, but the web will stay together. In fact, the rest of the web will be stronger after the few strands break, more able to flex without breaking so as to withstand the added stress. The spider, then, will only have to go back and repair the broken parts.

Put another way, the whole structure doesn't need to be deconstructed and then reconstructed, because there was nothing wrong with the whole structure; there was just something wrong in that one, localized spot. The spider—and you may relate to this—doesn't have the energy to start all over, again and again, every time one strand fails. So, too, our faith can be expected to change, in ways big and small, as our understandings of God, the Bible, and the world grow over time.

If our faith is a wall, and we learn something new that contradicts our old beliefs about God, we may think the whole thing needs to come down. But our faith isn't a wall; it's a web, and sometimes strands break and need to be replaced because they just aren't true, or because they just don't work anymore. We realize our ways of seeing God don't match reality. Our ways of experiencing God don't work like they used to. Our versions of gathered community and collective worship need reimagining. Those strands break, and we can rebuild new strands based on the other parts of the web that are still true, because the whole thing hasn't unraveled.

We may have grown up being told the Bible was trustworthy because of its literal accuracy. But then we hear sermons suggesting that biblical events are told in a style reflective of the ancient Near East, with its distinct literary styles and genres, meaning perhaps some events did not literally occur as described. The strand of literalism may break, but other strands—Scripture can be trusted, the God we meet in Scripture can be trusted—keep our web intact while we reweave our biblical perspective.

We might read Paul's words that "there is no longer Jew or Gentile, slave or free, male and female. For you are all one in Christ Jesus" (Gal. 3:28 NLT). But then we notice our church operates with hierarchy on the inside and also works to keep the wrong sorts on the outside. The "how church should work" strand faces stress as we discern whether we should stay and advocate for more inclusion, or go and change what form of community we're part of.

Or we may have grown up believing that "the ground is flat at the foot of the cross," and all are equal. But then we hear liberation theologians talking about God being especially on the side of the poor and the oppressed. Our wall didn't topple over; some needed tension got added to our web.

We may have a faith that includes God being a God of order, who commands us to respect laws and pray for government officials and such. But then theologians of color presented a God who desires to overturn the corrupt and oppressive structures of empire. Well, a few strands might need reweaving there.

Whatever tensions or breakages have occurred for you, a web reminds you that those occurrences are not only to be expected, but just might be an asset. Just as, according to our friends at MIT, "a spider web gets its strength from silk strands working together and their ability to stretch when stressed,"[6] so it is with our faith. New questions, information, experiences, both positive and painful, *will* cause strands to break. It's inevitable. They weren't working anymore. But the spider doesn't tear down the whole web and start a new one. It strings new threads where the old used to be, fresh and strong, and yet elastic.

If you feel stuck and unsure about what to build for your kids, it may be because you are thinking about structures. You feel like you have to give your kids a "firm foundation" that will never fail them.

But strands, not structures, are more aligned with how we actually know, and live, and change. They are more aligned with the complexity of our real world, and our real God. In the midst of your own changing faith, it may be time to see yourself as simply needing to reconstruct some, maybe even a lot, but not all, strands in a meant-to-stretch web. When a spider does that, they take time, methodically attending to a seemingly tiny and nearly invisible section. Perhaps your own expectations for scope and time could use that kind of scaling-down.

Moving away from the image of a structure has an additional benefit. See, when I set out to build a structure, I follow a blueprint, and it needs to be followed exactly. Blueprints are predetermined and the structure reflects that. For far too long, families have been given blueprints to create obedient, good children: daily dinnertime

---

6   Steven W. Cranford, Anna Tarakanova, Nicola M. Pugno, and Markus J. Buehler, "Nonlinear Material Behaviour of Spider Silk Yields Robust Webs," *Nature* 482 (2012): 72–76.

devotionals, extended bedtime prayers, weekly Sunday school attendance. The blueprint promises to build the exact right faith (and if a
child does not become obedient and good, it follows that the parent
is failing to effectively "disciple" them).

Most books like this focus on helping you move from blueprint
to reality. They assume the blueprint, and the structure it will create,
are good and will yield the right "results." The point of the book,
then, is to help you get with the one-size-fits-all-families program,
to give you tips for following the blueprint better. It focuses on precisely *how* your family should build.

This is not that book, because it is focused on *who* you are helping your child get to know, but assumes that *how* you do that will
be shaped by who your child and your family are. There are many
right ways to be a family of faith, but the right way for your family is
the one that works in your actual lives. So in this book, we are going
to talk about ways to weave a web that will be as unique as your
family is.

I'm not saying nothing in your life will ever have to change
for the sake of Jesus and the world he loves, but if the only people who can truly experience the promise of the gospel—freedom,
joy, peace, justice, life, and more—are the ones with enough time,
space, or money, the ones with kids who can sit still and memorize their verses, well, then a lot of us are out of luck. Far too
often, the blueprint claims to be one-size-fits-all, when in actuality
it's one-size-fits-some-mythical-family-with-lots-of-resources-and-
privilege.

Our faith is a web, not a wall, and as such it gets to take on
its own shape—a relief to many of us who didn't know there *were*
tangle webs until just now, but can kind of picture one based on the
name and know that's the shape our family needs.

Your role as a parent is to help your child weave their own web of faith, anchored to who God is, but with internal strands that take on the shape and texture that reflect your kid and your family, and this book can help you do just that.

Let's start weaving.

CHAPTER 2

Weave Your Own Web

For one particular research project, my colleagues and I at Fuller Youth Institute conducted long-form interviews with a number of families who had been nominated by their faith communities as exemplars. We asked pastors to nominate families based not on whether the kids "turned out right," whatever that might mean, but whether the families stayed faithful through the normal challenges of life, even as kids made mistakes and didn't unfailingly comply with their parents' wishes. They were doing something right because they kept figuring out how they, as the real family they were, followed Jesus and invited their kids to meaningfully join in.

There are two big things I want you to know about these interviews. First, almost none of these families did the same thing as another. Yes, each was in a faith community. Yes, each had a set of faith practices that included Scripture and prayer. But the type of faith community they were a part of, what they did to explore the Bible, and the way they approached prayer were all quite different. As they talked about their values as Christians, they certainly didn't sound identical.

They had found a way to live their faith as the family they were.

A quick story before I tell you the second thing about these families. When my youngest son was two, I tried CrossFit for the first time. I was looking for an exercise option that could be done first thing in the morning, and where if I showed up I wouldn't have to use my still-groggy brain too much because someone would just tell me what to do. Check and check. Early on, I learned there were "core movements" that worked the major muscle groups, like your quads. Then, there was "accessory work." Accessory work focused on the small muscles that were, well, accessories to the major ones. We might balance on one leg like a flamingo to work the tiny muscles that surround the knee and ankle, for instance.

Now, the second thing I want you to know about the exemplary families is that not one of them did devotionals, where all members of the family sat together for a time of study and discussion about the Bible. I know—did we EVEN talk with Christian parents at all? Don't get me wrong—they talked about the Bible—but the way they did so was tremendously varied. None of them accepted the cultural pressure to make the family devotional into the core movement, and anything else a family does to follow Jesus into accessory work.

Like CrossFit, Christian subculture has been willing to advise everyone of the list of core movements. From devotionals, to Scripture memorization, to weekly church attendance, we've been ready to prescribe the exact regimen every family should follow. Whether we're looking for it or not, whether our kids like it or not, whether it fits our family or not, we are expected, just as I am when I walk into the gym at 5:30 a.m., to do what we're told. In return, we're promised it works. And by "works" I mean it ensures that my kid will (a) be good, and (b) have a lifelong faith. The amount of emphasis placed on each activity varies by context, but there's a general two-part promise that this regimen will keep a kid out of trouble and "on the straight and narrow" as it were. (Interesting how the "narrow path" Jesus described was walked not by the moral, but by the trusting, and yet the phrase as we use it now is all about good behavior.)

This Christian subculture rests on two faulty assumptions. First, that someone else gets to determine for us what our family's core movements are; and, second, that family faith is one-size-fits-all, that there's a formula to follow, a program to adhere to, a single plan with no need of customization. In fact, most books for Christian parents exist to help you follow the formula, offering suggestions and hacks for how to get your family on track, with the unspoken starting point being that your family is very much off track. Since *of course* you need to do devotions, they have suggestions for how to make that happen. Since *of course* your kids need to memorize lots of Bible verses, they have tips to get them to stick.

CONSIDER

In what ways have you experienced the assumption
that your family's faith or your child's faith should look
a certain way? What forms or practices are expected?
What factors shape that assumption (relational, cultural,
denominational, etc.)?

Faith doesn't work by formula, so we are not going to either. Faith, as much as it pains me to say so, is not CrossFit, because God, I think it's safe to say, doesn't do burpees. And also doesn't boss us around. Which means I cannot dictate your core movements. This is another reason we are going to be guided by a spider's web: No two are alike. Each is a custom design reflecting not only the species of spider but also the environment in which the spider finds itself.

Did you know that the webs we often picture—shaped like a wagon wheel with threads connecting each spoke, like on the cover of this book—account for only 10 percent of all webs? Not only are there multiple basic templates for webs unique to the type of spider, each individual web has to adapt to its specific location, adjusting the details to accommodate the obstacles and contours of its place. Weaving a web is a unique, bespoke, creative activity.

The same should be true of a family's web of faith. So many factors impact the way faith takes shape in your family, including the number of family members and their ages; how your family earns an income; the location you call home; your personality, history, preferences, and heritage. All of these, and more, deserve to be factored in to how it looks for you to follow Jesus together. Being a family of faith, in other words, can and should also be a unique, bespoke, creative activity.

WEAVE YOUR OWN WEB

But you don't have to just take my word that nurturing faith happens in one hundred right ways, based on one hundred unique factors. There is, thankfully, non-spider-based research to back this up. As various groups have studied faith development and transmission in recent years, what they have found is not a set of universal faith practices for every kid and every family but broad themes, themes that are important but that can be brought to life in a variety of ways. The particulars are adaptable, not predetermined. The interviews I mentioned earlier highlighted that reality—each of these families had found amazing, Jesus-centered, life-giving ways to practice faith that fit who they were, and not one of them did that just like another.

One family described their core value of hospitality, lived out as they cleaned the house together each Friday for the express purpose of welcoming people over the weekend. They wanted to be able to spontaneously invite others over, knowing their space was ready to receive them. All this was explained to their kids by connecting the dots between the practice of keeping house and the immense welcome of God. They talked about their apartment as a gift and a refuge, and how important it was for it to feel inviting. Hosting people was not about living some Magnolia life; it was how they loved their neighbors. Thus, Friday night cleanup was a faith practice.

One family used the tradition of a summer road trip to visit relatives as a means to support being who God uniquely made each of them to be. Each family member got to design the itinerary for one day of the trip. On that day, everyone else went along with that person's choices for restaurants and an activity. They talked about the wonder of God's image in each person and how this was a fun way to see each member of the family just as God made them to be. Thus, a family trip was a faith ritual.

What about your family? What unique characteristics need to be accounted for as you craft a vision for faith?

- Who makes up your family? List the members. You may share a living space with them or not, live in the same town or not, be relationally close or not.
- Next to each person on the list, jot down a few distinguishing key traits of that person. What are they like? What are they interested in?
- What are some of your family's strengths and loves as a group? Do you love a good party? Cheer for a certain team? Love a particular place or meal?
- What are some of your family's unique challenges right now? Do you have a child who doesn't "fit the mold," for whatever reason? Are finances tight? Have any of the relationships been strained or broken?
- List anything else that feels important to you about who your family is and what they are like. What other traits make you, you?

Nurturing a faith that your child does not have to heal from happens as your family gets to be who it actually is. It's an ongoing process of answering the question: *How will* we *follow Jesus together?*

and establishing the habits and practices of faith that will make up your family's unique web.

I want to begin by highlighting four *un*helpful approaches to this process, because recognizing those from the outset can be so important in clarifying your own vision.

FOUR UNHELPFUL RESPONSES

Moralism

The first unhelpful answer, as I mentioned in chapter 1, is moralism. Moralism is, simply, making religion primarily about becoming a good person. Religious activity or involvement is treated as a tool to help a person be moral. Instead of asking, *How might we follow Jesus together?* moralism asks, *Can Christianity help me (or my kid) be a good person?*

Moralism often works like a contract: I am a good person, so the deity owes me safety and happiness. I'm good, so I deserve good things to happen. Moralism is the pseudo-Christian cousin to manifesting good vibes into the universe, or whatever. But moralism is often enforced through the threat of loss. If I am not a good person, then someone—the deity, the adult I love and depend upon, or both—will be less pleased with me.

Moralism can be built upon any list of dos and don'ts that mark what it means to be a "good person." The lists can be focused on personal virtue or societal ills. They can uphold so-called conservative or liberal values. But there are lists, and the religion of moralism maintains those lists.

Moralism tends to fail in the face of two realities: pain and exhaustion. When the moralist experiences pain, it leads them to conclude that either (a) this pain or hardship means I must not have been good after all; or (b) this deity must not be good after all, because they didn't honor *my* goodness by preventing this challenging situation. Exhaustion is related, as someone thinks, *Why am I working this hard to be good? Is this worth it?* If the only motivation for their effort is an abstract sense that their behavior pleases God, eventually list maintenance will be too tiring. This is as much true if the list focuses on personal holiness as if it focuses on social justice (both of which have a place in a holistic, healthy faith but must be given their home under the umbrella of the character of the God we trust).

Despite its shortcomings, contractual moralism is appealing. It asserts that one can control their happiness through their right behavior. It offers a path by which our children can avoid the hardship of consequences for poor choices. But it does so through a threat of loss, whether stated overtly or simply implied. God is happy if you are good and less happy if you are not good, and there's always a chance that you could be bad enough to lose God's favor. Moralism persists in part because of how it allows adults in authority to use a deity as leverage for compliance, which leads us to a related, but distinct and equally unhelpful friend: obedience training.

Obedience Training

Obedience training asks, *How can I make sure my kid obeys God?* Beyond simply hoping a kid will be good, like moralism does, obedience training tends to begin from the notion that the child is not good, but could become so as they learn to obey. It hopes a kid will be compliant to the requirements of the deity (and usually the deity wants the child to be compliant to the parent, which is a nice added bonus).

But our role is to offer kids a healthy, life-giving, love-filled space in which to grow. To bypass the process and jump straight to obedience is dictating, not discipling.

A literal disciple of Jesus went through a process of getting to know this new rabbi Jesus, listening to what he said and who he claimed to be, watching what signs he offered as proof of his authority, experiencing the fruit of his work over the years. They were figuring out who he was. What's more, these folks would have come to the process already prepped with a lifetime of Scripture knowledge, more aware of the details of their collective faith story than most of us will ever hope to be. Still, Jesus welcomed this process, walked with them literally and figuratively so that they could decide if he could be trusted. He invited them to obey as a sign of their trust, not instead of it.

Wait and See

A third unhelpful response is to wait, doing and saying very little about God or the Bible until a child is older. If you've been hurt by the way faith was presented to you, this can be especially appealing, because you don't want to pass along bad religion to your kid. If God or the Bible were weaponized against you, of course you might wonder if the best course of action is to steer clear until they are older. Or, this response might appeal because while you know what you don't want for your kids when it comes to faith, you're uncertain about what you do want. Perhaps you are hoping to be more personally settled when it comes to theological questions or biblical interpretation before opening yourself up to the questions (*so* many questions) your kids will have. You know that you don't have answers yet, and where will that leave you when the questions start rolling in?

These misgivings are totally understandable; it makes sense to have them when you're *so* wanting a faith your kids don't have to heal from. But I think, even so, that we need to engage on the topic of faith with our kids instead of waiting, for two important reasons. First, remember that we are not looking to replace our once-solid foundation with a new and improved foundation. It's not the case that, given enough time, we can find all the answers and thereby have immovable, earthquake-proof certainty to offer our kids. God, the Bible, and the world are too complex for the construction metaphor that leads us in search of certainty, and if certainty were required before introducing our kids to God, well, we might be waiting awhile. But a lack of certainty is not the same as having nothing to offer. We have the ability to be a companion to our children as they get to know God too. That's true even if we are learning alongside them.

Second, doing nothing isn't neutral. The myth of wait-and-see is that when you are ready to start talking about faith, your child will be an empty vessel, ready to be filled with ideas about God. The reality is that the core ideas kids have about faith, and life in general, are formed in the childhood years, and they are set primarily through the culture of the family. Life in a family, whatever its makeup, context, and culture, is formational. Kids learn some version of how the world works (for good or ill) early on, and any revisiting they do about core ideas will be done in dialogue with what was formed in childhood and adolescence.

If, as a kid, faith is about curiosity and wonder, if questions are asked, if God is trustworthy and it's okay to be working out what that means and looks like in a hard world, then, as a teen and adult, a person will tend to still think that faith can handle hard questions and that God will be with them as they work that out. On the other hand, if, as a kid, faith is dictated by adults, if questions are rejected or given pat answers, if faith expression is about list-keeping, that person's teen and adult years are likely to mirror that expression. In the case of the latter, this often yields either a rigid religiosity or an exhausted rebellion against keeping the lists just right.

But if, as a kid, a family ignores religion entirely, a kid will learn that faith is irrelevant when it comes to living a meaningful life, navigating its questions and ups and downs. They'll also receive messages from other sources—peers and other adults—without the same interpretive assistance that you could offer to help them assign meaning to what they've heard. They will be experiencing a religious formation of some sort, because your life together is a silent curriculum; *how you live* teaches them things about God, life, and the world. What you get to choose is whether you'll also talk about it together or it will just remain unspoken.

In other words, it is both that particular doctrinal statements or scriptural interpretations get passed along from adult to child *and* that the culture and posture of faith—curious or certain, consistent or sporadic, meaning-making or arbitrary—tend to get adopted by a kid. This will be true whether you do something intentional or passive as it relates to religious belief and practice. Your family's life together is a spiritual curriculum for your child. Both what you do and what you don't do communicate what is important and of value and what is not.

Being Reactive Instead of Intentional

The final unhelpful response is one we alluded to just now—to look at your own childhood experience and either copy it or do the opposite. The problem is that a reactionary approach, whether it was "I loved this and it worked for me!" or "I hated this and it didn't work for me," is not as helpful as an intentional one. You are reading this because you want to pick, on purpose, a way to be a family of faith. To copy or do the opposite of your own experience misses some essential elements of intentional faith parenting, namely:

Adjusting to Your Child's Unique Traits

Your child learns in their own way, at their own pace. They enjoy certain kinds of activities more than others. They have strengths and struggles all their own. Given this, it follows that how you help them get to know God should flow with the current of who they are. Take the practice of prayer, for instance. We've been telling kids to "fold their hands, bow their heads, and close their eyes" for a long time now. The point, I suppose, is to minimize distractions from the important conversation they are having with God. But there's no reason to require quiet stillness in particular, especially if your child would love to draw God a picture or finish a sentence you start for them (e.g., "Let's name people we love. Thank you, God, for…"). It's not only acceptable, it's preferable to find faith practices that can be adjusted to the kid you have.

Aligning with a Co-Parent

If you are raising your child with a co-parent, their story and preferences are also important when it comes to how you will, together, approach faith. How you'll go about introducing your child to God needs to be mutually agreed upon. You each may have strong preferences about certain things, but you must compromise and collaborate on this.

For instance, my husband and I grew up in very different church cultures. He was part of a traditional Presbyterian church, complete with organ and robes, whereas I was part of a contemporary American Baptist church that grew into a relatively smallish megachurch when I was about twelve. He was baptized as an infant, while I chose to be baptized in a backyard Jacuzzi when I was ten. Neither one of us automatically gets to decide if our kids will be baptized as infants or offered the choice later on, to use just one of many possible points of difference. It's a mutual decision.

Awareness That the Culture Today May Have Changed Since You Were Young

My first church job out of seminary was working with kids of middle and high school age. I remember one meeting with a fifteen-year-old girl and her grandparents, who were raising her after some hard circumstances made it impossible for her mother to do so. These circumstances were important in the girl's story, but as we talked, it became clear that the grandparents saw the teen's current struggles as purely connected to that piece of her situation. What they were missing, even as she explained it straight to them, was that she felt misunderstood. Not because of her mother, but because of the generational gap between her world and the world of her grandparents. She was a digital native, yet they expected her friends to call on the landline if they wanted to hang out, so they could also chat with those friends and get a feel for their trustworthiness. As a result, she felt socially disconnected and lonely, but her grandparents saw her social circle as rude and likely a poor influence on her. That perceived poor influence was especially important to them because they cared deeply about their granddaughter and were keenly aware that she'd faced hardship and needed support.

Our breakthrough moment came when I passed along a nugget Dr. Chap Clark was offering at the time to anyone who would listen. Chap, whose own research also focused on teens and faith, reminded us young seminarians in class one day that adults are inclined to tell kids, "I have been young and you have never been old." And kids tell us the truth in response: "You have never been young in the world I am young in, and you never will be."

I could see the relief spread over the granddaughter's face at having this named so succinctly. This was what she was trying to communicate. I could see the comprehension dawning on the grandparents' faces—their granddaughter wasn't trying to rebel; she was feeling misunderstood. We focused the remainder of our time on identifying several ways the norms for teens had changed. We didn't call the changes bad or good—those labels would have been counterproductive—we simply named them.

The changing culture for kids deserves our curiosity and continued learning. As we raise kids in a radically different world, we need not adjust to every new thing, jump in with every trend, trying oh so hard to be, like Amy Poehler in *Mean Girls*, "not like a regular mom." The choice is not between acquiescing to every cultural shift or being a mature guiding adult. That false dichotomy has contributed to a lack of curiosity, openness, and awareness about just how radically different the world for young people is compared to the one we grew up in. (And I say this as a millennial, the generation forever called lazy even though we're nearly forty, stable, and raising babies.) Instead, the better we understand the world of young people, the better we can support them as they navigate it, including what it might look like to trust Jesus.

CONSIDER

Which of these four less-helpful approaches has the strongest pull for you? Do you have a sense of why that may be?

FOUR HELPFUL ELEMENTS

Let's come back to our guiding image of a web. The variety that nature produces in web shape and function helps each unique spider survive and thrive in its particular context. What your family needs and what mine needs when it comes to how we follow Jesus can be remarkably different from one another. For instance, it happens that both my husband and I are only children. Given our extremely small extended family, we can approach Christmas and Easter with a lot of flexibility and freedom. Our traditions are largely within our control. This may not be the case for someone with a large extended family that gathers in particular ways, which will necessarily factor into their family's approach to faith around the holidays.

Put another way, there's a common aim we'll share for the remainder of this book. Rather than teaching you tips and tricks so that you, too, can conform to my predetermined core movements, what if we align around a larger, shared goal? What if we adopted the goal to

be with our kids as they get to know God and discover if God can be trusted.

To do this, you'll craft a family faith culture, an intentional set of habits and practices that help you live connected to God and what God is doing in your lives and the world. This is your web. This is a way of living your ordinary life joyfully and sustainably, aligned with God's character but in your own creative way, while at the same time not seeking to control your child's faith experience or force a specific outcome (mainly because that isn't actually possible, so this is just a way of recognizing your limits).

Your family needs a faith culture all its own, a way to joyfully and sustainably follow Jesus as a family and invite your kids along in intentional and meaningful ways. You need to weave your own web.

With this in mind, let's turn our attention to four specific elements that can inform and guide you as you're weaving the strands of that web: biblical exploration, experiences, rituals and traditions, and relationships.

Biblical Exploration

Biblical exploration is the category of practices that help our kids get to know God through the Bible. It includes the ways we tell stories, ask questions of the text, and discover God's character and actions through the story of Scripture. We help kids see that God is trustworthy now, in large part because of what God did then, and that God's fundamental attributes, attitudes, and aims for the world are unchanging. As with all these things, there is not one uniform approach that all kids or families should employ in order to explore the Bible. We will devote the next two chapters entirely to how to approach and explore the Bible with kids, so for now, I'll move on to the other three.

Experiences

Experiences help connect and counterbalance biblical exploration, extending faith into the wider world. They offer kids a variety of ways to connect with God and give them a chance to try different faith practices.

Faith experiences can take many forms, of course. One way you might think of them is that they are embodied and external—things we *do* more than things we think about or talk about. Though a person may reflect or discuss along the way, those aren't the main goals.

Rest and play during a Family Sabbath (more on this in chapter 5), generosity as we give time or money to address an injustice, worship and a chance to connect with God through music—all these and more create space for our kids to discover God beyond the world of words. Words are great, but if we aren't intentional, it's easy for the words of Bible stories and the words of prayers to make up a disproportionate amount of a child's faith sensibility. The fact is that the experiential *is* educational, and kids need the chance to live some things as much as they need the chance to hear or talk about others.

Experiences distinguish themselves from our third category, rituals and traditions, principally by being more sporadic in frequency.

Rituals and Traditions

Rituals and traditions are the things we say or do with our kids that get repeated, whether that repetition is daily, annually, or anything between. They may come from our tradition or faith communities, or we may create them just for our own family. Often they are connected to our schedule or calendars, such as:

- Meals
- Bedtime routines
- Words you say as your kids start the day, head to school, or return home

Rituals and traditions are often connected to the regular things a family inevitably navigates together:

- Family mantras can help us persevere through a challenge or remember who we are.
- A template can guide how you ask for and offer forgiveness to one another.

Some are born from a desire to lean into special experiences and connect them to important ideas:

- Holiday traditions for Christmas and Easter help us enter into God's great work in the world, not only as it happened in the past, but as it continues today.
- Birthday celebrations are a chance to bless a family member for simply being who they are, honoring them as a gift from God and expressing gratitude for them.

Repetition is the very thing that empowers any of these practices. Rituals and traditions might vary in intensity, duration, depth, and required effort (in fact, a great many of them will be low on all four of those things!), but in doing them again and again, a thread gets woven in a child's web.

Experiences and rituals are significant not only in providing space for distinct faith practices or learning, but also because these are the categories wherein you nurture faith by nurturing family warmth.

Family warmth is the sense of connection, support, and affection that is shared among members as they live together. Dr. Vern Bengtson of the University of Southern California highlighted the significance of family warmth as the single most important relationship factor in faith transmission. Of the many significant relationships a child will have—with teachers, coaches, mentors, and friends—family relationships will mark them most. When a family has nurtured warmth, the child is far more likely to share a desire to be part of the faith that family adhered to.

Warmth can be cultivated in myriad ways, but the key is the fuzz factor. Does it make your people feel warm fuzzies? Then lean in.

Relationships

The final element is **relationships**—with peers and adults in your kid's life who support them, and you, along the way. These could be friends, members of your faith community, teachers, coaches, or extended family. They could be people with you for a season or for the long haul. Whatever specific form they take, it's nearly impossible to overstate the significance of relationships to your child's faith. Our God, after all, is a relational God.

Research from Dr. Chap Clark, Dr. Kenda Creasy Dean, and the Sticky Faith Project from the Fuller Youth Institute all speak to the vital role a collection of adults can play in a child's faith. This body of research reminds us that any significant message will stick with a child much better if it's repeated by many different adults who are invested in the child's life.

I call this group "faith cheerleaders." These are adults other than yourself and your co-parent who

- basically align with your understanding of God, faith, and the Bible;
- are a consistent, positive part of your child's life (the specific frequency will vary, but consistency in their life is key); and
- you would trust to talk with your child about God, faith, or the Bible without you there.

It's not just that faith cheerleaders echo what's vital about faith to your child, it's that they engage in a meaningful, ongoing relationship with your child. The collective research on faith formation for young people draws out that intergenerational relationships play a key role in a kid's long-term faith. These adults do more than reinforce a message; they invest in your child as a whole person.

YOU ASK

My parents/in-laws approach faith very differently than we do. I know they love us, but I'm nervous to have them talk about God with my kid. What do I do?

It's obviously difficult to feel misaligned with loved ones on faith. The good news is that they could still be a faith cheerleader if what they echo for you are big themes, like God's love and grace. However, you may need to set boundaries around particular topics, like hell; practices, like whether your kids can visit their church; or products, like kids' Bibles. In that case, say something like, "We are grateful that you are part of the community who reflects God's love to our kiddo. Given that we don't see eye-to-eye on some of the ways our faith plays out, we need you to let us take the lead on how our kiddo hears about God or what's in the Bible. That means we hope [give specific examples of what's in-bounds, for example] you'll keep saying, 'I love you and God loves you more,' but you can't [name what's out-of-bounds, for example] keep criticizing them for not folding their hands and bowing their head just right during a predinner prayer."

Boundary-setting conversations are rarely our favorite, but be encouraged that the benefit for how your child gets to know God is worth it.

It's possible that this is the most challenging element for you. While the locus of control is your own, you can begin to envision how you'll craft a family faith culture. But once you need to incorporate others, things feel different. You simply may not have people in your life who could take on this role. The adults around your child may have such a vastly different understanding of faith that they seem like a risk, not an asset, to the faith-forming endeavor. For one reason or another, you might be starting from scratch, which can be overwhelming. May I encourage you that the effort is worthwhile? The relational threads you weave in this process could be the most wonderful element in the web. Faith cheerleaders support you and your child alike through life's inevitable highs and lows. They hold and honor hard questions, resisting tidy answers. They remind us that we belong to the family of God.

CONSIDER

Of the four helpful elements (Bible exploration, experiences, rituals and traditions, relationships), which one comes most easily to you right now? Which one are you most looking forward to nurturing even more?

Your family's unique faith culture is cultivated through a collection of habits and practices that invite your child to explore the Bible, have faith experiences, participate in rituals and traditions, and grow relationships across generations. The specific manner in which you implement these four categories will be uniquely your own, and helping you to discern how that will look is the purpose of this book.

To help, each chapter in part 2 will include a variety of ideas for practices you might incorporate to help your family weave your own web. You'll find specific experiences, rituals, traditions, and relationship-building ideas there. As for biblical exploration, you'll find a Bible story related to the attribute of God we're focused on, written the way I'd tell it to a kid and then unpacked for our purposes. I've also included a few questions meant to help you discern what fits for your kid and context. My encouragement is for you to answer these along the way, because our final chapter is a process by which you can bring everything together—ideas you loved, things you want to quit, family uniquenesses you want to honor, the whole shebang. By pausing to reflect as you go, I think you'll find that moving from ideas to action will be a far easier transition.

For now, let's start with you. Sure, you picked this book up for your kid. But your faith story matters for your family's web. It influences your child's own web. You personally may not have been given what you hope to give your own kid.

Given the aim to be with our kids as they get to know God and discover if God can be trusted, answer these questions:

How are you, personally, feeling about your own journey of knowing God and discovering God can be trusted? What impact might that have on weaving your own family's web? What might you need for yourself, even as you consider these ideas for your kids?

May the God who sees gossamer threads amid rosebushes and beneath brambles, calling them art, draw near to you, giving you a holy imagination for the unique shape your faith, your child's faith, and your family's faith could take. Amen.

CHAPTER 3

Do Less on Purpose

"Where are the dinosaurs in Genesis?" "Did God make sin, since God made everything?" "Why doesn't God just make mean people nice?" To state the obvious: Kids have a delightful curiosity about God, the Bible, and our larger faith story. They wonder about the details and ask about topics big and small.

The flip side of this delightful curiosity, of course, is that we have to answer.

The task of answering can bring up many feelings for us:

- Inadequacy about not knowing the Bible well enough
- Excitement to see our kids interested in faith for themselves

- Fear that the true answer is not appropriate to share, so now what?
- Hope for how these conversations over time will help them know God
- Pain stemming from how that question was handled when *we* asked it
- Pressure to ensure they accept the answer we give

So where are the dinosaurs in Genesis? To answer, you could tell a kid about the various ways Christians have approached this and related questions about the Genesis time line and creation. You could tell them Genesis 1 is a poem, and that the use of structure and flow is meant to show God's power to speak life, to order the world so it thrives. It tells us *that* God did it, but not *how* God did it. You could tell them the dinosaurs had already died by the time Genesis was written.

There are many ways you could answer. How do you choose how you will answer? I'd like to suggest that you do less, on purpose. Not just to answer faith questions, but as an overall strategy for faith content. And here's why.

MAXIMIZATION AND INFORMATION OVERLOAD

There are two cultural factors that can, without our even realizing it, shape our assumptions about how to approach faith content (Bible stories, theological ideas, and the like) with our kids. First, our culture tends to be obsessive about maximization and optimization, pushing for everything and everyone to always be the best that they can be. And then second, there's the very modern idea that if we just transfer enough information into someone's head, if people just know the Truth (with a capital *T*), then all that true information will result in changed behavior. These factors combine to create an expectation that kids should know as much Bible as they can as young as they can (and by extension start showing obedience as young as possible). If some Bible knowledge equals goodness, then more Bible knowledge equals extra-maximized goodness.

For instance, I once wrote about—and I'll share more about this in the next chapter—my belief that kids under age five only need to know that God is good. All our biblical stories, our prayers and songs, our key phrases about God, should be examples of that goodness. One person responded critically that their preschoolers can learn so much more than "God is good." "We can teach our kids all the basic doctrines such as: creation, sin, repentance, atonement, salvation, resurrection, and heaven," they wrote. In other words, we should teach kids the maximum amount of content possible at the minimum viable age.

While of course this parent is free to teach their three-year-old all those things, it raises the question for the rest of us: Should we? Is it better to be teaching preschoolers seven areas of doctrine instead of telling stories that exemplify one key attribute of God? If the goal were super-optimized three-year-olds, then sure, knock yourself out with the doctrine. If the goal is lifelong trust in a fundamentally good God, maybe hold off a bit. I say that not because doctrine isn't important, relevant, or perhaps even understandable to preschoolers, but because it's simply too much, too soon. It's information overload.

It's certainly true that kids can sincerely know and love God at a very young age. It's also true that there is a content element to faith formation. A child cannot get to know the person of God without also hearing the stories of Scripture, practicing connecting to God in prayer, or being offered substantive answers to their questions about God and the world. The problem arises when external metrics—how much content have they memorized?—overtake other important factors, like whether a kid understands or enjoys what they are participating in.

CONSIDER

How do you usually feel as you respond to your child's faith questions? List three to five key words.

Instead of maximization and information overload, we can do less on purpose by practicing spiral learning, using the skip-and-save approach, and practicing the three S's (smaller, shorter, slower).

WHAT IS SPIRAL LEARNING?

Spiral learning is an approach that can help us both be strategic about faith-related content and have a plan for engaging with a child's questions. Fair warning—or maybe you'll expect this by now—the strategy is intentionally smaller, slower, and shorter than we perhaps might have thought it should be.

Simply put, spiral learning is an educational strategy where teachers circle around important ideas again and again, over time, on purpose. Each time they return to an idea, they add something new onto what's been learned so far. It is especially useful when students need to learn something complicated or nuanced, because layers of complexity can be added with each spiral.

Given that faith is indeed complex and nuanced, we as parents can draw upon spiral learning in our approach to faith content and conversations. We approach the content that accompanies our faith—whether that content is the answer to a question or things we want our kids to know—with a spiral mindset. Rather than expecting a faith topic to be covered in a one-and-done approach, we should make the idea small, knowing we will circle around to it again (and again) to add information or a new layer of depth.

When educators talk about this idea, they remind us that kids are vital participants in the learning, offering what they already know, rather than being passive recipients of what the adults present to them. So, too, with us. Anytime we're in a faith conversation, our kids should do as much of the talking as possible.

You may be thinking, *Look, it's all well and good that* professional educators *know how to break down complex and nuanced ideas for kids. But I am a nonprofessional here, and while I know* that *faith is complex, I'm far from a master of those complexities.*

That's understandable, so let's turn our attention to how to spiral. Now that we know we are intentionally going to spiral and add complexity, the way we do that is to apply the principle of one truth, not one shot.

ONE TRUTH, NOT ONE SHOT

Spiral learning tells us that anytime our kids ask us a faith question, the answer we give is not the only, ultimate response for all time. This single conversation about God or the Bible is not your one shot.

So, when those delightful faith questions come your way, answer with one truth. Literally one. Tempting though it can be to cover all kinds of ideas when you explore a Bible story, name *one true thing* about who God is in the story. Rather than answering a complex question with every relevant detail, give *one key point.* There will always be more that could be said, but you save that for when you spiral around in the future. You stick to one truth, because this is not your one shot.

YOU ASK

I want to take this kind of approach with my kid's questions, but what if I just don't know the answer at all? What if I don't even have one truth to offer?

It can be nerve-racking to not know the answer, but let me encourage you: Your goal is not to have the answers. It's to create an environment that keeps inviting questions.

So here's one strategy you might try: First, say, "I don't know," and affirm the question as good and important. Be honest that you need more time to think about or need to learn a bit more about that. Second, search, either together or on your own, depending on their interest and the question being asked. Try to settle on a good answer. Not the best, most correct answer, just a good one. Third, circle back, adding what you learned, and then keep the conversation going by asking what they think of that new addition. Say, "I don't know," search, then circle back.

After limiting your response to one truth, invite your child's input. One key reason you limit to a single true idea is so your child can add on as much as they want. (This is that note from the educators in action about working with what your kid already knows or wonders.) Your child might notice a bunch more things. They might ask more questions and none of them seem to have anything to do with one another. (And again, you'll answer them with one truth.) By limiting your answer to just one truth, you are creating more space for your child to join the conversation.

You may now be asking: How do I pick that one truth? Here's a process to help you filter.

Something True, at Their Level, That You Can Build Upon Later

If I am writing curriculum, the first question I ask (or our team discusses) is always "What is one attribute of God we will highlight from this Bible story?" Every Bible story has many possible attributes of God to point out, so in order to effectively make it smaller, knowing we'll spiral around again, I take the approach of *focusing on something true, at their level, that I can build upon later.*

As a parent, you're not designing lessons, but you are trying to foster frequent, safe, natural conversations about God, faith, and the Bible. (What you are doing, by the way, is harder by far than scripting lessons that an experienced facilitator delivers.) And this filtering strategy can work for you too.

Let's look at an example of how this might play out using the story of Creation:

- **Possible truths:** God made everything; the world is diverse by design; humanity bears God's own image; we were made to partner with God so the world works in a way that matches who God is; God is three (especially when paired with John 1).

- **Filter by "at their level":** In this case, let's take the one truth that God made the world diverse by design. For kids ages two to four, that might sound like, "God made us different on purpose because it makes God happy."

- **How could you build on this later?** With a child who is around age seven, you might explore the question: What do our differences show us about who God is and what God is like? By the age of nine, you could discuss with them: How do you think God feels when some people are treated poorly for being different from those with the most power? Given how God feels, what might that mean for the people of God?

Filtering *something true, at their level, that you can build upon later* helps you strategically limit what you say to your child so that you stay within their developmental capacity. It's how I decide what I say about those pesky missing dinosaurs.

If we don't pick just one thing, many times kids will simply shut down, saying it makes sense whether it does or not, or get frustrated, because the grown-up is answering a question they aren't asking as they add on extra facts or details. If we aren't at their level, they'll be bored or it'll go over their heads. If we don't intend to build later, we miss the chance to spiral around the idea so that it can deepen for them as they grow.

Try it: Pick a Bible story you personally love. List some possible truths that come through that story. Filter them

to the level your own kid(s) can access. Can you imagine adding on in the future when they are older? You're doing it! Remember, this approach can also help you answer your child's faith questions or approach other theological ideas.

When It's Still Too Much: The Three S's (Smaller, Shorter, Slower)

What if you are trying to keep faith conversations short and focused, but you find that it still feels like too much? You are trying to spiral, you know you have more than one shot, but it's not quite clicking. It's possible you might still be expecting too much from your kid, in which case it can help to consider how you'll scale down. One of three areas is often the key:

- **Smaller: Reduce the amount of content.** Spiral learning breaks concepts down into many very small, often simple, pieces. Perhaps you are still trying to cover too much. A whole story, plus a related memory verse, plus a prayer might be more than your kiddo can do at one time. Maybe you just talk about the story, and on a different day you tell them about that verse. Doing less is not lower quality, because the goal is not to check the "Talked About God" box. The goal is for your child to fully engage and enjoy the conversation, because engagement and enjoyment both support their learning.
- **Shorter: Reduce the conversation length.** A good conversation (or other faith-related activity) can go bad if it's pushed beyond its time cap, which is set by your kid's engagement. (*Engagement*, remember, goes beyond

listening. Let's say you decide to make a card for a sick friend. The timer begins as soon as you introduce that idea to your child. The time they spend thinking of what to draw, imagining how the card show's God's love, and listening to you is all part of the activity. If you try, after all that, to also tell them a story about Jesus helping a sick person, you're likely past the time cap.) What's more, your child may engage for a long time on some occasions, but just a short time on another. They may talk a lot one day in the car, but when you try out a new bedtime reflection question, they've got nothing. A basic rule of thumb is that a child can engage with something for about two to three minutes times their age, meaning the attention span for various ages is, roughly:

- two years old: four to six minutes
- three years old: six to nine minutes
- four years old: eight to twelve minutes
- five to six years old: twelve to eighteen minutes
- seven to eight years old: sixteen to twenty-four minutes
- nine to ten years old: twenty to thirty minutes
- eleven to twelve years old: twenty-five to thirty-five minutes

Again, just because a child might be able to engage for a certain length of time does not mean that maximum time is the goal. Pushing a child to the edge of their capacity may change an activity from fun to a slog, whereas wrapping up sooner keeps it enjoyable.

Slower: Reduce the frequency of the practice or activity. Maybe you've got the right environment for faith conversations (the car, the breakfast table, after lights-out at bedtime) but the wrong frequency; and doing the same thing, but less often, will work better. You don't have to talk about God every day. You want to be talking about God regularly and consistently. But your kid may need more time between conversations to process ideas, form questions, or simply come back around to the topic. As I mentioned in the previous chapter, your family will have a web of faith that includes experiences, rituals, and traditions as well, and those will be happening in addition to overt conversations, supporting them in faith as well.

THE SKIP-AND-SAVE APPROACH

As you begin to practice filtering the content that is at your child's level, you'll be left with some topics or Bible stories that you think are not a fit, but perhaps have commonly been presented to kids in other contexts you've been a part of. Violent stories are one example of this, as our culture often thinks kids (especially boys) will find battles and killing to be adventurous. There are those who assert that these things need to be shared with children anyway, that since they are the truth (sorry, Truth, capital *T*), a child simply needs to know. I disagree, owing to the reality that the Bible is not fundamentally a children's book. I think not only that you can but that you should skip the content and Bible stories that are not at your child's level (again, *your child's*. Maybe another seven-year-old can engage in a certain topic, and yours can't. You know your child's level. And remember, our goal is faith development in the long run, not which seven-year-old can do the most).

Consider the story of Noah and the flood. It's often included in children's Bibles, Sunday school lessons, and nursery wallpaper patterns. It's the story of how almost everyone on earth died, including all the cutie-patootie creatures, and yet we tell it to toddlers, because "Awww, look at the cutie-patootie creatures!" Yet even just that snapshot of the passage (of which scholars have devoted entire books) helps us see that this story becomes kid-accessible only when a child is older, making it a prime candidate for the principle of skip and save.

In order to begin to understand the story, a person has to be familiar with the real, awful, painful effects of sin. They have to know the abhorrent things humanity is capable of. They have to be able to empathize with the grief God feels to watch the world work in ways that are fundamentally opposite of God's character. If I just stopped there, that would be reason enough to skip this story with young children. Most simply do not know this about the world yet. (And the ones who do know it are living it, meaning that tender compassion, support, and resources for healing are what they need, not the telling of a story that will certainly confuse them about whether God cares about them.)

Next, it's helpful to know at least a bit about the genre of the story so that we're aware of how the original hearers were likely to understand this account. For instance, in the worldview of ancient Israel, what made God good was not God's ability to support individual human flourishing—this concept that is so removed from how we often view God that it's hard for us to imagine. Nevertheless, we have to try to see that for the original audience, a god is good if they are able to make order out of chaos. Chaos is the enemy, because it wreaks havoc, violence, and death. If the weather behaves chaotically, for instance, crops do not grow and people starve. The god who is powerful and trustworthy is the one who can overcome and order the chaos, and—here's the thing—if individuals, even a lot of them, die for that order to come, they would not have seen any conflict with that god still being good. The god just did what they had to do to bring the good of order. As hard as it might be for us to wrap our minds around it, this was simply the paradigm by which they evaluated these things.

YOU ASK

I know that the Bible's context and genre are important, but I don't always know how to learn about them so I can help my kid. How do I try to take these into account before I talk about the Bible with my kid?

I always say you don't need a seminary degree to talk to your kids about Jesus, but I understand why it can feel like you do. There are a few books that can help you get the lay of the land when it comes to context, such as John Goldingay's *A Reader's Guide to the Bible* or Rachel Held Evans's *Inspired*. For specific books of the Bible, I love the series The Bible for Everyone. But if that's still more than you can do, here are a few very basic things to keep in mind:

- The Bible is neither a history textbook nor a science textbook according to the modern sensibilities of history and science. The writers were not concerned with telling every event as it literally happened. So as you read, bear in mind that there would have been a culturally embedded style for telling stories, one that everyone then would have understood. Knowing there is a style helps, even if you aren't familiar with its intricacies.

- The world of the Bible was culturally collective rather than individualistic. By thinking about how a group would engage the text, we move toward it.

- God's character is consistent. While storytelling styles vary and poetry and symbolism fill the pages of Scripture (at times creating confusion for us), God's character serves as our anchor. And if we find ourselves losing track of who God is, we look at Jesus.

- At times, that seems to be the problem, though—God doesn't seem to be good in the way we think God should be. As this comes up, try asking yourself: Although this seems troubling to me now, in this time and place, how might it have been comforting or helpful in their time and place? Make your best guess and allow that to lead you forward in peeling away the layers of the story.

Trying to wrap our minds around such a fundamentally different worldview is likely to be difficult for us adults to consider as readers of Scripture; it'll be even harder, if not impossible, for a child. But without this peek into the very different time, place, and culture that carried this story, we won't see it in the way the writer hopes. Only as we know this type of thing can we begin to recognize that this was a story of God giving undeserved grace in saving Noah's family and continuing to offer humanity the chance to partner in the filling and beautifying of the world. This is Creation 2.0 as far as Israel is concerned, and a sign that God kept God's promises.

It's also a story that can't be told on its terms until a child is older, so we skip it and save it for later.

Saving some Bible stories until kids are older respects both their unique development and the Bible itself. It respects your kid as someone who can meet God, grow into understanding the story of our faith, and not be pressured to "get it" by some deadline. It respects the Bible as a book whose faithful testimony of who God is comes through a story told in a context, a genre, a culture, and a specific moment in history.

One key to knowing if you should share or skip a story is this: *If you can't tell an accurate version of a Bible story in a kid-accessible way, skip the story. Save it until you can.*

Now, one could change the meaning of the story in order to present kids with some sort of message. This is certainly true if the person wants to promote obedience, because Noah obeyed and the other people disobeyed. But it's hardly appropriate, nor is it most aligned with the passage, to tell a child that God drowned people who didn't follow God's rules. That is simply kidifying a story, and there is a difference between kid-accessible and kidified.

KID-ACCESSIBLE VERSUS KIDIFIED

A kid-accessible story is one we can share with a child at their level. When we make an idea kid-accessible, we may do things like choose simpler words, or summarize a story rather than read it verbatim from the Bible. When deciding what it means to be at a kid's level, this is what we're thinking of: *Can I be faithful to the story's meaning but present it to a child?*

But when a story is kidified, the meaning gets changed from something authentic to the passage to something different (often something that suits the agenda of the adult). Kidifying is a helpful tactic for obedience training. Almost any Bible story can be lifted from its time, place, and genre and converted into an admonishment to "be good." One famous, beloved, produce-based cartoon occasionally kidified Bible stories, resulting in those stories being told entirely different from their actual meaning. For instance, David and Bathsheba was reduced to "Don't be jealous." That's… not quite the point. But the transformation of a story about power abuse, sorrow, the power of God's faithfulness and grace, and yes, a bit of jealousy, into simply "Don't be jealous" is kidification.

Noah, as I mentioned, is often kidified into "Obey God, even if other people think you're weird." Jacob and Esau are kidified into "Having siblings is hard, but God can help you get along." (I also saw "We should love our brothers and sisters" to go along with Cain and Abel. Again…not quite the point.) Baby Moses being put in a basket as a last hope gets kidified into "Families help one another."

Kidifying a story often leads to a time when a young person returns to the Bible, reads a story for themselves, and thinks, *Wait, what?!* What they were taught has little to do with what is actually going on. The result is not only confusing, but also compromises the trust they have in the adults who introduced God and the Bible to them.

As parents, one way we can assess if a Bible story or other faith concept is at our child's level is by asking ourselves: *Am I making this idea kid-accessible? Or would I need to kidify this to make it understandable to them?* If the answer is the latter, then we skip and save that story or idea for a future time. It will become something we add as we spiral, helping us build on ideas we've introduced earlier.

BRINGING IT TOGETHER: CONVERSATIONS THAT WORK

Now that you have a basic understanding of why and how you might do less on purpose—using spiral learning; filtering to one truth, at their level, that you can build on later; and using the three S's if it still seems like too much—let's turn our attention to how you, as a parent, might form an intentional approach to the Bible for your family.

Wait a second—you said I didn't have to do devotionals! That I did. You don't need to force your kids to talk about the Bible at a particular time of day, using a particular curriculum, for a specific length of time. (I hear a lot of people thinking it has to be during dinner at the table, for twenty minutes, for instance.) I hope you will, however, talk about the Bible with your kids, and find a rhythm for biblical exploration together. That usually means one of the following:

- Picking a time of day that fits for your kids, when they are most relaxed and conversational. Maybe it's the drive to school or practice or maybe it's sitting at the breakfast table. Maybe it really is dinnertime for your people. My older son talks most in the last ten minutes of the day, during the comically misnamed part of our routine called "Quiet Time." It's just him and my husband; lights have gone off, and that's when all the questions and thoughts pour out.

- Picking a way to tell the story that your kids enjoy and can understand. That might be a children's Bible, or it could mean you as the storyteller; it could mean listening to the story on a podcast, or they could read a story from a Bible themselves.[7]

- Using these strategies to limit what you point out, leaving lots of space for what they notice.

We'll talk more about what exactly you'll do as you engage with a specific Bible story in the next chapter.

For now, may I say again: I hope you do less on purpose. Less can give you more. Less content at one sitting for the purpose of more, real learning over time. Less talking by the grown-up for the purpose of more talking by the child. Less time all at once for the purpose of more time again and again later.

Less in the short term gives you more in the long term. And this—nurturing faith by engaging with its content—is a long-term thing.

CONSIDER

Where might you be able to do less on purpose? What kind of less—less content, less length, less often—might actually give you more faith conversation overall?

---

[7] My personal preference for a Bible translation if a kid is going to read the story themselves is the New Living Translation.

CHAPTER 4

About the Bible

I remember the first lesson I ever taught to kids. They were in grades four through six. I was sixteen years old. The lesson was about patience, and to illustrate *im*patience, I took a bite out of an orange without peeling it.

Gross, but certainly not the grossest thing I've done for kids.

I've done this bit where you spit a grape to a friend who catches it…in their mouth. Then they spit it back and you catch it in your mouth. Back and forth.

I've eaten a live worm. A small one, but still.

Then there's this one where a person brushes their teeth, rinses with water from a cup, and leaves it there for someone else, who brushes their teeth and leaves the water in the cup for someone, who also brushes their teeth. At the end someone brushes, but instead of following suit and spitting into the cup, they drink the water.

I've been the last person in that bit. Yet, for some reason my husband still kisses me.

With that orange-chomping lesson marking the beginning, I've been deeply involved in ministry to children since 1998. At the risk of sounding like Paul detailing his Pharisaic bona fides, I joined Fuller Youth Institute as a research assistant in 2007, giving me the chance to better connect with the data on faith formation in young people. I grew up on Sunday school, complete with snack time and flannelgraphs. I've put on big, mega-fun events for kids and families. Throughout the years, I've written curriculum for kids from age two through age twelve. Point is, I've been around the block a bit in churches, long enough to see various approaches rise and fade when it comes to how we help kids know and follow God.

The reason this is relevant to our discussion about faith and parenting is that understanding some of this history can give us insight into why it's so challenging to do something as seemingly simple as talk about Bible stories with our children. So, if you'll indulge me, I'd like to help us get our bearings a bit in the history of kids' church ministry in the US over the past seventy-five years or so. It'll be a quick walk-through, I promise, and then I'll show you how it relates to spinning a web of faith that works for your family.

In a very broad sense, you'll find two major perspectives shaping children's faith curriculum: One emphasizes biblical information—knowing not only the plot of Bible stories, but the details, often accompanied by an emphasis on Scripture memorization. This approach has been the opposite of "do less on purpose."

The other major perspective emphasizes biblical application—telling a child how the principle of a Bible story should be lived out in various everyday situations.

If you've ever tried to buy a children's Bible or devotional, chances are good that you've had an experience with one or the other of these perspectives, though you may not have had this context to draw upon. Titles emphasize the character trait that will be featured as your child hears the story of a particular human from the Bible. But that is precisely what makes them unhelpful to our goal of helping our kids get to know God. One is too focused on the plot details and the other is too focused on the people. Allow me to explain.

Those focused primarily on biblical information tend to think that what adults are most meant to do is *educate* children about God and the Bible. Often, that education is accomplished by listening to an adult, the teacher. A child's role is to receive what is taught and adhere to it. Stylistically, this group also tends to buy into the idea that Christian formation is best done via classroom learning.

The myth that God is best learned about in a classroom developed in part because in the 1950s, Pastor Henrietta Mears from Hollywood Presbyterian Church first put kids into Sunday school classes by grade. Her purpose was to offer kids the chance to meet God in ways created just for them—for their age and their level. She recognized that kids have unique needs that couldn't be met in the pews of "big church," with its grown-up language and liturgy (though the value of being part of the larger church family is unquestionably important).

Sadly, over time churches held on to the form of the classroom, but forgot the real reason kids were given those classes to begin with: to discover God as the kids they were. As our understanding of childhood development and learning increased, our strategies for helping kids learn about and know God could have adjusted accordingly. Instead, we invested more and more in an informational approach, giving kids bricks for their walls of faith each week, trusting that if we built the walls strong enough they wouldn't someday topple over.

Those focused primarily on biblical application (a more recent development beginning around 1990) felt the need for a more interactive and engaging style as they also questioned if biblical knowledge was the ultimate goal. They wondered, *Is this information yielding transformation?* This group agreed that it mattered for kids to know the Bible, but they most wanted kids to apply the Bible to their lives, knowing what to do in various situations because of it. For five years I worked as curriculum director in the kids' ministry of Willow Creek Community Church in the Chicago area. Prior to my arrival, Willow wrote and sold its curriculum, and every lesson had three aims: *Know What* (what will a child learn); *So What* (what, specifically, did it mean to them? Notably, this was prescribed, not discovered by the child); and *Now What* (what, specifically, will the child do this week in light of the other two. This was also prescribed).

I understand that the intention of focusing on biblical application was a good one: The Bible is relevant to the life of a child; God cares about the life of a child; we should help kids know what it looks like to live biblically in their world of classrooms and sports teams and siblings. The breakdown comes in the way this approach presented Bible stories, tending to look to the human characters in order to determine if they did what was right or not. Were they heroes to be copied or antiheroes to be learned from?

This led to lessons with main points like the following:

- Be faithful like Abraham.
- Be brave like Esther.
- Be patient like Joseph.

To illustrate this further, let's use the example of David and Goliath in 1 Samuel 17, since it's a story many of us are at least a bit familiar with.

God's people, the Israelites, had gone to war with their enemy the Philistines. But for forty days they had been at an impasse because the Philistines had offered a challenge: Send the best soldier out to fight their own best soldier, in a winner-takes-all, man-to-man battle to the death.

The problem, of course, was that their champion was a giant. (Maybe not literally, however. Did you know that portraying one's enemies as gargantuan is a common feature of stories from the ancient Near East? For other nuggets of contextual insight, may I recommend Dr. John Walton, whose series The Lost World is incredibly helpful for better understanding the Old Testament's various genres.)

First, we'll approach this by putting the humans in the center of the story, so we start by talking about how the Israelites got it all wrong for being afraid. They didn't have enough faith in God; they weren't trusting enough. Lesson one: Don't be like those Israelites.

And then, if we are trying to learn from the humans of the story, it continues like this:

One day David came to bring his brothers some lunch and heard the taunts from the giant. He approached the king and said, "Who is this man who insults our God? I will fight him for you." David was brave. He gathered five stones from the stream. And then David courageously went out to face the giant.

Lesson two: Be like David. Trust God; be courageous.

Then David faces Goliath, saying, "I come before you in the name of the God of Israel." He loads the slingshot, sends a rock soaring, and down goes the giant.

And God?

God in this story is an observer, judging the merits of the various actions the human characters take. God is proud of David for being courageous and having great faith. God is disappointed with the Israelites for cowering at the Philistines.

In this model, a kid is supposed to apply what they heard by being like the human hero, courageous and ready to defend God's honor. But what if they don't? What if they can't? What then?

We see again in this example how this style of teaching reinforces rather than corrects the messages of contractual moralism. In telling kids to be like David, the focus shifts away from the uniquely grace-based gospel that aligns with the story of Scripture and toward a moralistic contract wherein David received God's help because of his own goodness.

Speaking of David's "goodness," he wasn't so good. If you're familiar with David's fuller story, you see power abuse, assault, and murder.

He was a terrible father. Why the label "man after God's own heart," then? Because of trust. David returned to Yahweh God, again and again, instead of trusting idols. Apparently, God can work with that. This is, incidentally, what God-centered storytelling, which I'll outline later in this chapter, opens up for us with older kids. They can hear the (paraphrased) story of David and Bathsheba, because the purpose is to discover what God is like. They discover a God who can redeem terrible situations, who does not leave us when we make huge mistakes, who ensures our story is never over as we come back to God, again.

Approaching the story in this manner basically communicates to kids that God is also a bystander in their own lives. God watches them, evaluates their choices, and likes them a little bit more or a little bit less depending on whether they get it right or not. If God likes them, they might slay giants; if not, they're in trouble.

To be clear, the problem with emphasizing biblical application is not the desire for relevance, but how the tactic devolves quickly into moralism. By focusing on whether the humans were or were not obedient, and therefore whether a child should or should not emulate them, the takeaway for the child is meant to be, "I should be faithful. I should be brave. I should be patient." In other words, "I should be a good kid." Implicit is the idea that being a good kid makes God happy, and if God is happy with me, then God will make my life happy in return.

This message often gets reinforced by offering kids a principle, derived from the story, that they are meant to remember. "Biblical principles" sound good—portable nuggets of truth that go with our children wherever they go. But to get to the principles often involves disconnecting from the bigger narrative of Scripture. The Bible story just becomes supporting evidence for the principle. But I could use a historical hero just as well as a biblical character and get to the same conclusion. Be faithful like Gandhi. Be brave like Harriet Tubman. Be patient like Disneyland ride operators in the late afternoon when kids should be napping but want to get on the Snow White mine train.

The biggest problem with mining Bible stories for so-called "biblical principles" is that this simply isn't what the Bible is about. The point of the Bible is not to provide principles, but to tell the story of what God is doing in the world. Real, regular humans are important characters in this story, but God is the central character throughout.

Perhaps it's more accurate to say that whatever principles emerge from Scripture, they are based not on the behavior of the humans but on the character of God. The "principle" of generosity is based on the generosity of God; the "principle" of patience is based on the patience of God. They are integrally connected. We are invited through the stories to put our trust, exclusively and entirely, in God, who is generous, patient, and so much else.

A tweet I saw a couple of years back captures all this and can offer a case study to us. It was posted by a pastor with a large following, who said, "No matter how smart or successful we become, we're always susceptible to forsaking basic biblical principles we learned as kids. If our convictions change when the culture turns up the heat, then we never fully internalized the moral from the three Hebrew boys and the fiery furnace."

This captures the following assumptions:

- Bible stories have morals to hold on to, like "Don't let your convictions change when the culture turns up the heat."
- The purpose of childhood is to load up on these biblical

principles. This will equip a child for adulthood, where they should be loyal to said principles.

Another consideration with biblical-application-focused resources is how they reinforce moralism in the way they give kids a clear, specific action item to do, prescribing the way they will apply the principle to their lives. This makes the next step from the lesson clear and concrete, something every child is meant to do, often within the next week. Examples of prescribed applications include things like this: Pick someone in your family and do something to help them; or, the next time you see someone being treated unkindly, step in and stand up for them. While of course these could be offered to kids as options or ideas, the more common occurrence in the model is for these next steps to be dictated to kids.

You may be familiar with the elementary school program "Character Counts." It begins with a character trait—honesty or respect, for instance—then it tells stories to kids about people who were honest or respectful, so that they, too, can go be honest and respectful. Kids are given activities where they draw a picture of a way they can be honest. They circle answers on a worksheet that are examples of respect. The point is to be an example of that trait. Prescribed application in kids' Bible conversations is basically "Character Counts," but Christian, reinforcing the notion that God mostly wants a child to be good and is pleased when they are. Put another way, these prescribed actions tend to become the very things that populate a young person's religious dos and don'ts lists, like we talked about in chapter 1.

What I'm arguing is that children are better served by an approach that does three things:

- enters each biblical story in its historical context first, instead of trying to mine the story for a timeless principle;
- helps kids understand who God is, instead of focusing on the humans; and
- invites them to respond to the story without a single prescribed application.

So, in the case of those "three Hebrew boys," Shadrach, Meshach, and Abednego, if we mine their story for principles, we come up with something like, "You should stand up for God no matter what and God will always take care of you!" But if we first enter the story in its context, we start with the backdrop of exile. This was devastating to God's people, disorienting and confusing. When a conquering king took over, that was seen as a sign that their god(s) were stronger than your god(s). The Hebrew people were facing the decision: Do we continue to trust Yahweh God, even here? Even now? Or should we bow to the gods of Babylon, and Nebuchadnezzar their king? Are those gods stronger?

The choice is: Who will we trust to protect and provide for us? And standing up is the answer: We will trust Yahweh God of Israel. Shadrach, Meshach, and Abednego admit they might die, but even so they're making that choice to trust. Even if it doesn't "work," meaning that God does not save them in the way they hope, they aren't going to change course.

This is important to the story: There are things about God's character that these three draw upon to make their choice. The amazing display of protection offered in the midst of the fire is important, but they made the choice without knowing the outcome. They weren't adhering to principles; they were standing on the trust they held in the person of Yahweh. We might ask kids: *What do you think helped them decide what to do? What did they know about God? What stories were they remembering from the past?*

Entering the story this way allows for the three men to be more than heroes. They can be scared. They can be confused. They can be unsure. They can remind us of what we all face when our circumstances make it feel like God is not powerful or present.

Instead of telling kids to stand, we can invite them to reflect on times they've felt like these men must have felt: *Have you ever felt like God was far away, even if you also want to trust that God is close? Have you ever had a time when things were bad, but you've also been told God is good? What happened? How'd you feel?*

Embedded in all of those sample questions is the idea that the child is an equal participant in responding to the story and to who God is. Instead of a prescribed application, the conversation is oriented around helping a child take a next right step, without predetermining what that step will be.

This alternative approach can be summarized in this way:

God-Centered Storytelling: We should practice interpreting Bible stories for kids through the lens of God as the main character and for the purpose of discovering who God is and what God is like.

Explore and Respond: We explore Bible stories with our kids and invite them to respond to what they notice in them.

I'm going to explain this approach more fully, but rest assured that in part 2 of this book we will practice how this is done in every chapter. Specifically, for every attribute of God that we will consider together, I've selected one Bible story that shines light on how God is that way. We'll practice God-centered storytelling, as well as explore and respond together.

GOD-CENTERED STORYTELLING

When we are introducing our kids to the Bible, we have to understand that all Bible stories for children are interpreted. This is good; this is how it should be. Interpretation is how we move from the level of what happens in a story to the level of what the story means. What makes things complicated is that there are many different approaches to interpretation, some far better than others, and Christians disagree wildly, and emphatically at times, about which are best.

Biblical interpretation can be literal, metaphorical, allegorical, moralistic, highly connected to the original context (or not), highly aware of literary genre (or not), or any combination of those, just to name a few.

I've mentioned before how I differ from those who believe the goal of Christian parenting is cultivating obedience in kids. One of the reasons we land in such different places is that there's a fundamental divergence between us in how we approach the Bible. Simply put, we interpret it in fundamentally different ways, which impacts both how we see individual verses and how we summarize the overarching narratives. This, then, impacts what we think is the best way to tell a Bible story to a child.

Most importantly, I think God, not humans, should be at the center of any story we tell to kids, the one around whom every other event or human action revolves. Every story includes a cast of characters made up of humans, God, and sometimes other aspects of creation, but when we tell a story, we should first look at how God feels, how God responds, and what attribute of God we see highlighted in this particular encounter.

God-centered storytelling looks at Abraham and says: God is faithful. God keeps God's promises. God never gives up on us. God made a family to show God's goodness to the world. It looks at Esther and says: God is at work even when we don't see God. God saves God's people. God is just, even when the wrong people seem to have all the power. God-centered storytelling looks at Joseph and says: God is with us, all the time. God can bring good out of bad. (And the bad gets to be truly bad. When Joe says, "God intended it for good," he's speaking to God's ability to bring good out of what was actually bad, not that the bad doesn't count because it was ultimately redeemed.)

God-centered storytelling is an interpretive framework, a lens through which we see the story. Its strength lies in three things:

- Its alignment with the aims of the biblical writers. This is the story the Bible is actually telling us. The writers want us as readers to see certain things about who God is and what God is like, and focusing on the humans often pulls us away from their original goal.
- Its ability to let the humans be fully human, rather than boxing them into hero/antihero categories. Certainly, sometimes the people in a story "get it right," trusting God and letting that trust lead them forward. But when the humans don't have to be heroes anymore, it's also okay for them to fail, to fear, to fall away. In fact, we will likely connect more effectively to the people in the biblical stories by inviting their fully human experience into the narrative. These are not robots or ciphers; they're actual, human people like us.

- Its ability to reach kids in a wider variety of experiences. When I tell a child to be brave or be patient, they may not actually have the capacity to follow through, for a variety of reasons. In that case, the story becomes irrelevant to them. In my experience a child often won't share that aloud. They will play along on the outside, saying the right things, while quietly determining on the inside that this faith might not really be for them, especially the more times they experience stories this way.

But if I tell a child about who God is, that truth is always accessible and relevant, because what I want to know is not *Do you believe that and agree with me?* but rather *When I say God is X, how does that make you feel? Is that easy or hard to believe right now? Why? Have you ever experienced God as X before? What happened?* These questions don't have right or wrong, pass or fail answers. Any kid can answer them in a way that's truthful. It just takes adults who are brave enough to slow down to the child's pace, who will be with a child while they express their trust and their barriers to trust without reacting in a way that causes the child to shut down.

With God-centered storytelling as our interpretive framework, we can then use the specific approach of **explore and respond**.

EXPLORE AND RESPOND

Explore and respond describes how we actually interact with Bible stories. We first explore the story with kids and then invite them to respond to what they notice in that story.

The Basics: Think Nature Guide

Both parts, *explore* and *respond*, have a key question that guides them. But first I want you to imagine that you plan to go on a nature walk in a new location. You're interested in the plants and animals that call this place home, so you decide you'd like to be accompanied by a guide. I studied abroad in Costa Rica for a semester and at one point went on exactly such a walk in a section of rain forest. Our guide not only helped us see tiny, jewel-toned frogs on trees, but also warned us to give a wide berth to the highly venomous snake coiled up and resting on a rock just to the side of our path.

A good nature guide will point out significant things to you. They'll also help you avoid major risks or pitfalls. And, there are things a good guide does *not* do. They don't overwhelm you with too much information. They don't control your whole walk, but allow you to linger where you're interested or move past things that don't capture you. They leave a lot of space for you to discover on your own. A good guide is a companion, but they are not controlling. They may know a lot, but they often hold back on purpose so you can notice things for yourself.

When it comes to our kids, we are trying to be good guides. We don't want to control, but at the same time our involvement is critical. We are companions to our kids on their faith journey, including how they explore biblical content.

As a guide, then, the key question of **explore** is: What does this story say about who God is or what God does?

As you explore a story, you might do the following:

• Read, paraphrase, or listen to a Bible story.

- Look for who God is and what God is like.
- Offer a key detail about the context of the story to help it make more sense in our time.
- Invite interruptions from your kid and encourage their questions.
- Notice the emotions of God and the humans at different points along the way.
- See if you can connect pieces of this story to other stories in the Bible.
- Try asking one question, such as:
    ◦ What was your favorite part of this story?
    ◦ What was the strangest part of this story to you?
    ◦ How do you think people felt at the beginning, the middle, and the end?
    ◦ What did you notice about who God is or what God's like in this story?

Remember our example story of David and Goliath? How does it sound when you explore the story using a God-centered storytelling approach?

It might shift like this: *God's people had spent the past forty days afraid. They'd gone to battle against the Philistines, only to become stuck in what seemed an impossible challenge: face the Philistine champion in a winner-take-all duel to the death. And their champion was a huge, terrible, terrifying giant named Goliath.*

But God is with us, even when things are scary and hard. The Israelites didn't know it yet, but God was going to help.

When God is the center of the story, it's okay to be afraid. The Israelites aren't doing anything wrong; they are just being…people.

You can ask your own child: What's something that makes you feel afraid?

One day David came to the battlefield to see his brothers. He heard the taunts of the giant; he saw the fear in the army. And David remembered God is with us—like the time God had been with him when he fought a bear. David remembered that God is greater than anyone, even if it doesn't feel like it. So, David said he would fight Goliath.

He gathered five stones at the river and then went before Goliath. Listen to what David said about who God is: "The whole world will know that there is a God in Israel... The LORD saves; for the battle is the LORD's, and [God] will give all of you into our hands" (1 Sam. 17:46–47 NIV).

David loaded the slingshot, sent a rock soaring, and down went the giant. God was with David. God saved the people.

You could ask your kid: What do you think David knew about God that helped him face Goliath while he was so afraid? Is there anything you know about God that might help when you're afraid?

With God-centered storytelling, the hero in the story is not David; it's God.

The hero throughout the biblical narrative is God. Even when God partners with people, they are not accomplishing anything beyond that which the Spirit of God enables and equips them to do. In other words, they stay regular, ordinary people who trust an extraordinary God. They practice trusting God in their circumstances, learning what that means both by doing it well and, just as often, doing it poorly. It's what God did in them, with them, and for them that we want our kids to see. God who can be trusted, God who draws near, God who cares. God who came in Jesus as hero, though in ways no one expected.

Picking Which Bible Stories to Explore: A Quick Guide to the Bible by Age

AGES ONE THROUGH FIVE: FOCUS ON GOD'S GOODNESS

First, when it comes to kids and the Bible, I believe we should always start with God's goodness (a trait we'll explore in depth in chapter 5). This is true if you are starting out with a very young child, or starting afresh with faith conversations with older kids. From birth through about age five, kids only need to hear about the ways that God is good. And regardless of the age of the child, if they are new to God and the Bible, this is the place to start. The style in which you highlight this attribute will be different for a preschooler than an older child, but the basic approach is the same. Select stories that exemplify that goodness in various concrete ways, then cite the examples as you explore the story. In other words, don't only say generically that God is good, but show, specifically, the form that goodness takes, such as feeding, listening, and helping.

Need some ideas to get started? Here are five stories to help kids anchor to a God who is good. I've phrased a key idea for kids five and younger. For an older child, you could also point out the same truth in a more suitable style.

- Creation—Genesis 1: What a good world God made! God made you good!
- Manna and Water in the Wilderness—Exodus 16–17: God took care of the people with food and water.
- Elijah and the Widow—1 Kings 17:7–16: God sent Elijah to help the woman. God helps us!
- Jesus and the Children—Luke 18: Jesus told the kids "Come to me," and he said they mattered very much to God. You matter to God too!
- Peter in Prison—Acts 12:1–18: God hears our prayers.

AGES SIX THROUGH NINE: EXPAND THE STORY

As kids start to move into the young elementary ages, it's a great time to expand from focusing on God's goodness to noticing what God is like as you explore lots of Bible stories. Kids in this season are story sponges, soaking up events, characters, and details. Given that, this is a great few years to focus most on knowing the smaller stories of the Bible, connecting the dots between Bible stories, and highlighting the single overarching story of Scripture. Don't get locked into Genesis-Revelation order; start with the stories you think your kid will enjoy the most and jump around. The goal is just to expand the story for them bit by bit.

AGES TEN THROUGH TWELVE: FOLLOW THEIR LEAD

At around age ten or so, depending on the child, it's a great time to move from just exploring Bible stories to looking to the Bible based on the topics and questions your kid raises. The questions or topics of interest to older kids often fall into bigger buckets like...

- What beliefs define our faith?
- How can we notice God's activity around us?
- What might trust in God look like in this situation?
- How can I get to know God for myself?

The key shift in later childhood is that it starts with *them*—their experiences, emotions, and questions. This is the beginning of connecting the Bible to their everyday life, because adolescence is the season when most young people are ready to take on personal application. It's not that there is never a time to ask a young person to think about how the Bible applies to their life. It's that having the capacity for introspection, emotional articulation, and greater individuation and autonomy all help them answer that question for themselves, instead of just saying what they think an adult hopes to hear.

After an exploratory conversation, the next step of the approach is to help a child **respond** using this key question: As I consider how God is X, or does Y, what would I like to say or do now?

Responses can take many different forms. A child might:

- Share a doubt or question
- Make art, sing, or dance around
- Share how they're feeling and why
- Show kindness or care for someone else

- Try a Christian practice like lectio divina or imaginative prayer
- Talk to God

And yes, at times, a child might:

- Take a step of faith in action

Notice that obedience has a home in this framework. It lives within response practices oriented around connecting with God. There are times a child will have a sense from the Holy Spirit that there is something for them to do in light of who God is or what God has done. The specifics of that leading will be as vast for a child as they are for us as adults: from invisible personal choices to visible acts that we might be privileged to witness.

What's important to note, though, is, first, that obedience is not the only good response, nor is it the "goal" response. It is one of many, with each being important in a child's growing faith. Second, obedience is the secondary response to an understanding of God's character. Only after having the chance to explore the biblical text with an eye for the attributes and actions of God does a child then consider what that might mean for them.

This means that we, as guiding adults, don't "begin with the end in mind," hiding in plain sight an agenda of prescribed and predetermined obedience. Instead, we're present with our kids, and also God, open to the specific and unique actions that are theirs to take. We practice being adults who trust God to lead our kids at the best pace for who they are.

The combination of God-centered storytelling with an explore-and-respond approach is what allows us to enter into the world of the Bible and connect it to the world today—both the wider world and the somewhat more localized world our children inhabit. It's one way we can help our kids weave anchor strands affixed to who God is, because they discover more and more about God every time.

Try it. Pick one of your favorite Bible stories and ask the following questions:

How does that story sound when the humans are made the center of it? What kinds of prescribed application ideas go along with that story?

How does the story sound if you take a God-centered storytelling approach? What do you notice about God? The humans?

What is one thing you, personally, want to say or do in response to that story? Is there a question you're carrying? Something you want to express to God? Someone you know who'd be good to connect with? Do you want to write, draw, dance, sing, walk, breathe, lie down?

PART II

In part 1, we focused on the *what*—what elements nurture a child's faith and form your family faith culture, namely biblical exploration, experiences, rituals and traditions, and relationships. In part 2, we will focus on the *how*—how those elements will take shape in your family to form your unique web.

As I said before, if faith is a web, its strongest anchor strands, the ones that give it structure, are connected to who God is. As parents, then, we help our kids discover who God is, what God's like, so they can establish those anchor strands for themselves over time.

The first six chapters in part 2, then, are oriented around who God is, specifically that God is good, powerful, just, joyful, and present, and Jesus is Lord. I selected these six because they are accessible for children across a wide age range, they speak to common questions kids ask, and collectively they help kids begin to realize God's complexity. These form anchor points and have important tension with one another.

It nearly goes without saying that these six attributes are not comprehensive and that there would be others you might wish to include as your child gets to know God. What these chapters will do is give us practice with a process of moving from the attribute, to Scripture, to practices in our everyday lives. You can apply the same process to characteristics of God that go beyond this book (and I'll talk more about that in the last chapter as well).

Every chapter devotes some time to defining the attribute, because it's not enough to simply say God is good; we need to help kids know what we mean when we say God is good. The same is true when we say God is just, or God is near, or anything else we claim is true of God's character. Using one Bible story as an entry point for deeper exploration (told the way I would to a kid, so you can hear how exploratory, God-centered storytelling might sound), we'll clarify what, specifically, we are hoping our kids see about that attribute.

Then I've provided a variety of ideas for experiences, traditions, and practices that you might try to help your child anchor to that particular element of God's character. The idea is not that you will do every one, but that they will serve as a beginning point and spark ideas of your own. I can't wait for you to get to the final chapter, because I've created a process for you to intentionally move from all these ideas to the select few that are best for you and your kids.

CHAPTER 5

God Is Good

The soft warmth of the morning sun spread like a golden blanket across my shoulders as I filled my lungs with salty air. Ocean air, I decided, was a bit thicker than the dry, hot air farther inland, where we lived.

Where we lived.

The delightful reality still hadn't fully settled in. We lived here again, back home in California, after five years in the suburbs of Chicago. Instead of the seemingly endless winter already lurking on the horizon, we lived where the horizon was the flat, blue line of the ocean, sparkling like glitter, dotted with ships waiting to be let into the nearby port.

My younger son, Peyton, was born in Chicago, so while he'd delighted in our excursions to Lake Michigan, the fact was he'd never been to the beach. Not really. (There is an explosive, years-deep conflict raging between my husband and me as to whether a narrow length of sand that happens to sit next to a Great Lake is a beach. To me, sand and water smushed together do not a beach make. The sounds and smells are all wrong, for one thing, and you can't surf on it. So, while it's beautiful—the town of Ludington on the coast of Michigan comes highly recommended—I maintain that the proper term for that beauty is "the lake," not "the beach." Now that we've got that cleared up, on we go.)

This was the beach. My absolute favorite place. As I took in the reality of our first time being here together as a family, I couldn't believe how much of God's goodness was crammed into this moment. The joy, the abundance, the beauty, the grace, the *life*.

I look now at the video on my phone of Peyton's first run into the ocean. He charges down to the water, accelerating as his feet reach the firmer wet sand, then makes a sharp U-turn as the first wave gets near his feet, not ready for the chill. He stops, looks straight at me, and calls, "Mommy! Come on!" before U-turning again and skipping back to the waves.

The video stops, but I have no difficulty remembering what I did next. I stopped recording, tucked my phone into the shady corner of our turquoise beach tent, stood up, and ran to the water.

That morning at the beach, it wasn't just generically nice to be there. As Peyton danced with the surf for the first time, it was specific evidence of God's goodness to us. Our feet sank down as the undertow pulled the sand away, settling us more deeply into the truth that our God is good, not generically, but specifically. This is the very reality our kids first need to experience, anchoring their first strand of faith.

Fortunately, this goodness surrounds us, taking many forms, expressing itself through God listening, providing, forgiving, and, most of all, loving right in the midst of our everyday lives. As adults, we might think of these various expressions of goodness as their own, distinct attributes of God's character. For children, however, especially young ones, it can be simpler to understand goodness as the reason God is or does any of those other things. While a day at the beach may not be the exact mechanism by which your child anchors to God's goodness, chances are that goodness will be discovered as much in the world God made as within the pages of the Bible or the walls of a local church.

Goodness is like an umbrella over all these other wonderful characteristics of God. In the mind of a child, who is often sorting the world into categories, with good and bad being an essential pair, the other characteristics are evidence of goodness. God is good *because* God cares, God listens, and God provides.

Which means that, when it comes to their web of faith, a child can first anchor to a God who is good, and then, as they grow, can add the nuance of God's compassion or God's wisdom, or any other characteristic that is both an expression of goodness and a trait of its own. They aren't anchoring to goodness and not love. God is good because God is love, and God is love because God is good. These kinds of particulars will become clearer to kids both as they age and as they get to know God.

There is another reason I'm starting with God's goodness. It's where the Bible starts. Before the world existed, God existed, which means love and goodness have always been, and will always be. And to emphasize this point, the creation narrative declares, over and over again, "God is good. God is good. God is good."

When I tell kids the creation story from Genesis 1–2, I tell it like this:

In the beginning, God created the heavens and the earth. There had been nothing at all, and God's Spirit hovered over the waters. Then God said, "Let there be light, and there was light."

God spoke and there was...

Light and dark.

Day and night.

God spoke and sky and land were made.

God spoke and plants were made.

The sun, moon, and stars.

God spoke and land animals, birds, and ocean creatures were made.

Every time, God says just a word and things are made. God can create with just Their voice. God speaks, and there is goodness all around.

We know it's good because there used to be chaos, but God gave things order. There used to be emptiness, but God started filling it up. For the people who first knew God and gave us God's story in the Bible, these were clues that led to a very important truth.

That truth matters for you and me now just as much as it did then, and it's this: Yahweh God is good.

Just look! Look at how the world came together under the goodness of God's creative voice. Look at how it all happens in such a lovely, orderly way.

Now here's something else: God's people lived together in one place, but all around them were other groups of people. Those groups had stories too. Every group had a story about who made the world and how they did it. Many of their stories went something like this: The world was made when the gods got into a great big fight. The god who won split open the god who lost, stretched Their body out tight, and that's what holds up the sky.

That sure sounds different from our story, so far. Yahweh God just needed to say the word, and the world became. Yahweh God made a good world full of good things. Why? Because Yahweh God is a good God. God could only make a world that matched who God is.

The Bible tells the creation story differently on purpose, because our God is different from those other gods.

A sky filled with birds, fields filled with grass and animals to munch on it, oceans filled with fish. Good, good, and good. But something is missing.

People.

God said: "Let us make people in our image, according to our likeness. Let them rule over the fish of the sea, over the birds of the sky, over the cattle and over the earth, and over every creepy thing that creeps along the earth."

So God created people in God's own image. In the image of God, God created them.

People are made last in this special poem, because people are special. Have you heard someone say, "Save the best for last" before? That's happening here. God saved the best for last. The whole world God made was good. But people? People are called "very good" by God.

* * *

This is our first Bible-story-as-case-study, so let's begin with the questions that face us as adults in a story like this, such as: *What if there isn't a literal Adam and Eve?* Or: *How much should I work on aligning this story with scientific thinking on the origins of the world?* Our questions are always worthy of our time and energy, but it can also be helpful to be aware of common pitfalls that leave us further away from the purpose and meaning of the passage, because that can help us prioritize our questions.

As I mentioned in chapter 4, with all Bible stories our primary question should not be: What facts or principles can I learn? Instead, we want to enter the story in its context in order to help connect it to ours. This is still true when we want to pass along the story to our kids, because chances are good that the writer of that story didn't set out to convey facts or principles in the first place. Instead, our first question should be: What does this story say about who God is and what God is up to? What does it tell us about God's character?

When it comes to the creation narrative, we as listeners are invited to discover that God is good. Not generically good, but specifically so. The writer isn't simply saying, "Isn't it neat that God made the world?" They are intentionally highlighting how Yahweh God's goodness is expressed.

You've heard the stories of the nations, they'd say. The stories of a world that was formed through battles and bloodshed, as the gods fought to be the ultimate? The stories that tell us that power expressed through violence is the way the world was given order and how that order is now maintained? Not so with our God. Our God used words alone to bring order to the chaos. God spoke out the structures that were needed—depths to brim with water, heights to be covered in snow, plains to be filled with grass. Then God spoke creatures to dwell in each one, a home suited just for them. The bright blue sky is held up not by the split-open skin of a defeated enemy, but by the word "up."

Now we may not have heard those stories. Their very existence may be a new revelation to us. But to an ancient ear, the creation narrative meant in no uncertain terms that this God is unlike the other gods, not only in Their power to create with a word, but in the goodness God brought forth with those words. This is why, for instance, it can be helpful to share with our kids that to people who lived in the world of the Bible, each nation had gods they worshipped. Not only will the creation story make more sense, but the whole narrative of Scripture becomes clearer as we understand how often the writers were fleshing out what it meant to trust Yahweh God and not the idols and gods of the nations. If we've always operated from the assumption that there is one true God, it can feel unfamiliar when the Bible seems to legitimize the existence of other gods. Much of the biblical story is oriented around the ways Yahweh was distinct from the gods of the nations, and whether those gods are real, just less strong and good than Yahweh, or whether those gods are nonexistent is actually a bit blurry. Nevertheless, the writers are often making their point to people who assume there are many gods, making it a critical point to share if we want to enter these stories in their context.

Back to the creation story, then. The world overflows with goodness because the God who made the world is abundantly good. That's a God worth anchoring to, worth putting trust in.

The writer of Genesis 1 was not commissioned to write a science textbook; they were inspired to tell us something deeply true about who God is. These are not the same thing. Is a science textbook one way to write something true? Absolutely. Is it the only way? No, thank God. I'm hearing "Amens!" from those of you who stopped studying science somewhere around high school chemistry.

Similarly, they weren't commissioned to tell a literal history that accounts for every literal person. Perhaps you've encountered scholars who note that Adam and Eve, rather than being literal people, are representatives of humanity. This aligns with how ancient Near Eastern narratives took shape and used symbolism. We aren't meant to try to figure out how their sons, Cain and Abel, had kids, given that no other women are mentioned in the early chapters of Genesis. We are meant to understand where humanity stands in the eyes of God: beloved, made in God's own image, intended to exercise dominion over the earth because God invited them to do so, and so on.

SPIRAL THE STORY

In addition to focusing on God's goodness, here are some ideas for spiraling back to the creation narrative with a God-centered storytelling approach:

- God made the world diverse by design. God seems to have set up creation to maximize the variations of life that would fill it over time. God made everything and everyone different on purpose because it makes God happy. Talk about ways that creation and people are different and unique.

- God is creative. Have fun noticing how delightfully odd some creatures are. Search "weird animals" online and marvel at the images that come up.
- God partners with people. The blessing to fill and rule the earth shows how God's first choice is to be on a team with people to make the world work in a way that matches who God is.

Again, I want to emphasize that God is not some generic goodness, like a kindly grandmother who always has a Depression glass bowl full of Werther's Originals by the couch. The writer of Genesis 1 wanted us to know what God's goodness looked like, what it consisted of, how it expressed itself in the world. And it's worth our looking briefly at some of those specifics now.

ORDERING CHAOS

In the ancient Near East, a major paradigm for goodness was whether something was orderly. Unpredictability = Bad. Chaos = Worse. Order = Good. Marie Kondo would have fit right in.

The creation story is carefully organized to show God ordering things. On days one through three, God creates good structures for elements of creation: day and night, water and sky, land and sea. Each is a container, and on days four through six, God fills those containers: the sun, moon, and stars; birds and fish; land animals. The days are not there to tell us what literally happened in a twenty-four-hour period (three of which come before the source of twenty-four-hour days, the sun, even appears). The days are there as a literary device to show us something far more deeply, powerfully, and importantly true: how God's order, and therefore God's goodness, spreads throughout creation.

Giving Life

The world God makes is designed for life to not only be sustained, but expanded and diversified. Creature after creature is told to be fruitful and multiply and fill the earth. The picture of God is of a life-giver, an *abundant* life-giver, a God who wants life to fill every square inch of this amazing creation.

This would be especially important when the gods of the other nations around Israel were, at times, life-takers (the practice of child sacrifice, which Yahweh God routinely calls abhorrent, comes to mind). Beyond creation, God as life-giver echoes for the rest of the story of Scripture, both in pragmatic examples like God providing food and water for the people of Israel in the desert, and in deeper examples, like God coming in Christ to defeat the power of death itself.

Image-Bearers

In the Genesis story, human beings are made in God's own image. This has many implications for our identity, including our own goodness and belovedness, the power we are given to reflect God to the world, and the role we can play as God's representatives in creation.

The idea of being made in God's image is not wholly unique to the Bible, though. Other ancient Near Eastern creation stories contain a similar theme, with one notable distinction. Instead of *all* humanity being image-bearers, as in Genesis, *one* human is an image-bearer: the king. The king is the reflection and representative of the gods, which is kind of a convenient story for the king to tell, don't you think? Because then the rest of the people have no choice but to serve the king in order to please the gods.

Delight

God calls creation good. Creation, all of it, delights God. What God has made is not for the purpose of making God comfortable, which is how many ancient cultures thought of things. Creation, in those stories, exists to provide food, comfort, and cheap labor for the gods, and any mistake could mean the end for us because of drought, famine, or infertility caused by the gods we've angered.

But in Genesis, God's posture toward creation is delight. God's position on humanity is approval. God is so delighted by creation that God shares power with them, so that they can complete this good world with their own creative flourishes. They can "exercise dominion" over it (instead of just living with God exercising dominion over them) because they are "very good."

Rest

We live in a culture that sees productivity as good and rest as, well, suspect. Rest is seen as, if not simply bad, then at best for the purpose of recovering so we can return to productivity again. In Genesis 1, though, God's rest is good in and of itself, and God is good because God rests. Consider again the gods of the nations, who demand work from their human subjects, all the time and at any cost. The writer differentiates Yahweh God as one who rests, and then invites humans to rest as well.

What we discover in this story, as we focus our attention on God's character, is overwhelming, abundant goodness. That's what Genesis 1 says about God, and from that we find that it's a story that also says so much about us. Our identity is tied up in this goodness too. When we anchor to the goodness of this God, we receive the invitation to join in God's rest as well as God's activity.

ANCHORING TO A GOD WHO IS GOOD

In the case of Genesis 1, a "faith means building a wall" approach collects the "bricks" of literal biblical interpretation, where kids are given a specific time line of creation. Each event is slotted in to show how God made the world in seven, literal, twenty-four-hour days (don't forget those dinosaurs!). But, as we've hinted at already, applying literalism to this story actually obscures what Genesis is trying to show us about who God is. It ignores genre (Genesis 1 is poetic) and context (the writer is intentionally distinguishing Yahweh God of Israel from the gods of the nations and those other creation stories) and elevates the mechanics of creation over the character of the Creator.

But it is precisely the character of the Creator that matters most in this story. The combination of reading stories like this well, and then going beyond the walls, literally, to experience the goodness of creation firsthand is what allows our kids to know and trust that God is good. In giving them the chance to connect the truths of the story to the wider world around them, we give them the chance to anchor to a good God.

CONSIDER

Which of the aspects of God's goodness have been most important for you? How has that changed in different seasons of your life?

What are some places, activities, or experiences that most help you truly experience God's goodness?

Which aspects of God's goodness do you most want your kids to connect to?

How might it look to anchor to God's goodness in everyday life? Let's consider some possible practices:

CREATION CARE

Inviting our kids to care for creation helps them connect to the goodness of "exercising dominion" well. They experience their power to steward God's creation, to make good in the world that God made good first.

Now, often at this point someone suggests a garden as a potential place to bring this to life. And if you have a garden and like to garden, then of course that's a great option. But some of us feel supremely *dis*connected from God's good creation when we try to nurture tiny plants to life. I once worked at a church that invited kids to help sprout seedlings that would be transferred to the church garden. The church garden was large, well cared for, and beautiful, and its produce supplemented a grocery distribution site for many families in our community.

The vision of including kids in the much-needed seed starting phase was a terrific one…except that kids (as you may have noticed) are not always great at daily, ongoing tasks that cannot be forgotten or missed. You know, like growing a plant from a seed. We passed out three thousand or so seedling kits, feeling optimistic that kids would love it and realistic that perhaps two hundred would come back to us. Want to guess how many actually were returned? Not two hundred: twenty.

What, then, are some *other* ways kids might engage in creation care, for the black-thumbed and forgetful among us?

- Bring a trash bag with you when you go on a hike or to the beach, and pick up the litter that you pass as you go. You don't need to turn your day out into a cleanup day, just grab what you can on the way.
- Compost your veggie scraps at home. Basic composting does not smell or attract animals (as the large pile behind our shed will attest). Composting can be done with just a small amount of food scraps, and kids can incorporate the sorting habit into their regular dish cleanup routine.
- Become members of a zoological or botanical society near you, and allow your visits to foster curiosity and a greater understanding of conservation efforts. We spent a couple of years as members of the Los Angeles Zoo, whose efforts played a significant role in reviving the California condor population. In a condor-themed imagination play space, my kids learned about the work the scientists did, and were left feeling hopeful about how humans can help animals.

- Enjoy a conservation-themed podcast or show for kids. Podcasts like *Earth Ranger Emma* or shows like the *Wild Kratts* are full of interesting facts about animals and often have simple ways kids can be part of habitat conservation without making them feel afraid or guilty about the more challenging parts of this work.

THE RITUAL OF LIFE-GIVING WORDS

God's words create life in the world, and our own words get to echo that function. As we speak to our children in life-giving ways, they internalize messages that align with who God made them to be, reinforcing the truth that they are made with care and deeply loved. It can be especially valuable to make these life-giving words into a ritual, where you say the same thing over and over again. Will they roll their eyes at you sometimes? Naturally. Will they remember? If you keep it up, certainly.

Here are three opportunities to build a ritual of life-giving words.

Bedtime

Chances are, your child has some sort of bedtime routine to help them not only avoid cavities but also get ready to sleep. As they end their day, kids are often overtired and overstimulated, though they may not have words for what they feel. You, then, can begin a ritual of speaking words of assurance to them. This quiet space invites them to rest their bodies and know that no matter what happened to them in their day, *here* they are safe. Here they are loved. The writer of Psalm 16 speaks of how their "body rests secure," because

Yahweh God is with them. At bedtime, you can be the one to vocalize this for your child. Here are two examples:

> You are safe. You are loved. I will see you first thing in the morning.

> Time to rest your body, mind, and heart in the unchanging truth that you are wonderfully made and dearly loved by God and by me.

Off to School

Anytime our children head off into the world on their own, we get to say one last thing to them. Since we'll be saying goodbye anyway, we can do so in a way that speaks to their identities as beloved and good. I know a mom who said a short prayer for each of her sons before they headed out the door for class. One dad had a nickname for his daughter that captured his affection for her, and he made sure to call her by that name before she opened the car door at drop-off. It's an opportunity to send them out with a reminder of what's most true about who they are and lets them know how you feel about them:

- You are a gift and a joy, and just who God made you to be.
- God made you kind. God made you good. God made you YOU.

Bumpy Days

When my younger son was five, we had a doozy of a day. The particulars blur, but the highlights were yelling (both of us) and biting (just him, but don't think I wasn't tempted). When calm was finally, blessedly, restored, I had a choice to make. What words would I say to help him make sense of the past couple of hours? Have you ever had the experience where you *really* needed God to give you that wisdom They promise to give, and it actually showed up, right on cue? This was one of those for me as I tucked his body in close, sniffed his salty-sweet head, and said, "Bumpy day, huh?" His body went soft into mine, and from then on we've used the phrase "bumpy" to describe times when we've struggled to treat each other well.

The obedience-training paradigm has a tendency to resist apologizing to children, seeing that as something only kids do when they've disobeyed. However, our apologies to kids are one way we "submit to one another out of reverence for Christ" (Eph. 5:21 NIV). If we as adults have dishonored the image of God in our children with how we've spoken to them or reacted to their behavior, of course we apologize, modeling the way of mending and forgiveness.

On bumpy days we may not be enjoying the ride, but we are still together in the (metaphorical, but sometimes literal) car, and still moving forward. (As an only child, I spent my childhood in the middle seat in the back of the car, loving my view out the windshield. Now, that seat is perpetually empty, because physically touching your brother can, shall we say, contribute to the bumpiness of the ride.)

Bumpy days are when we need words of grace and unconditionality for our kids. They are the days when a template for mending and seeking forgiveness can be incredibly helpful.

- God is the always-forgiver. I will always forgive you. Will you forgive me too?
- Nothing you do makes me love you less. Nothing you do makes me love you more. I love you so much, all the time, no matter what.

As we speak life-giving words to our children, over and over again, we offer our kids a connection to a God who doesn't just love them, but *is* love. Their identity, then, isn't just loved by you, but also loved by God.

Delighting in Nature's Beauty

Ours is a family of early risers, a state of affairs I have just had to make my peace with in the years since our kids arrived. It's not uncommon for our whole family to be piled in bed playing word games on various devices as the sun comes up. If the sky is particularly lovely, whoever sees it first will inevitably call out, "Ooh, look at the sunrise!" and we will all raise our faces to our bedroom's east-facing window to take in the orange, fuschia, and pale lavender streaking across the sky. When it comes to the beauty of nature, I find it never gets old. Every now and then, as we welcome the morning this way, my husband or I will say, "God could have chosen to start the day any way They wanted to. Isn't it great that God chose the most beautiful option?"

Noticing beauty comes fairly easily to children, given the

chance. Whether it's marveling at the size of a boulder, or taking in the colors of a changing season, kids are eager to say, "Wow" to the world God made. We, then, have an opportunity to anchor them to God's goodness by saying "Wow" with them. As an added bonus, trying to consciously engage with my kids on this level has opened up for me so much of the astounding detail and grandeur of creation that I had long since stopped noticing for myself.

Pastor Ben Patterson says, "Wonder is rooted in deep reverence for the God who made all things." It follows, then, that the ordinary acts of rolling down a grassy hill, finding shapes in the clouds, or examining the spots on a ladybug can anchor our kids to the goodness of God.

Family Sabbath

Taking a cue from the goodness of rest, your family could build a rhythm of Sabbath together. Simply put, Sabbath is when we "have nowhere we have to go and nothing we have to do," as Pastor Jeff Manion puts it, and instead we rest and play together. For most of us that isn't going to just happen on its own, but will instead require some preparation.

How might you begin this practice? The first tool you can use is your calendar. Put a chunk of time down for Family Sabbath and protect it. That chunk could be an evening, a half-day, or a full day, depending on what's realistic for you in this season. Maybe it starts small before growing over time.

Next, consider what must be done ahead of time knowing that you will be stopping for a while, and make those essential preparations. What needs to get cleaned up, set up, closed out, or turned off so that your Family Sabbath can actually be rest?

I thought I had a modicum of understanding on this, until I found myself, one Friday evening, halfway around the world in the home of a rabbi and his family on Shabbat. I'd traveled to Israel/ Palestine with a group from our church for the purpose of better understanding the region's conflicts and the work of peacemaking, which included the opportunity to celebrate this meal together. It was so much more than a meal, of course, evidenced by a level of preparation that boggled my mind. Each dish was warmed on a hot plate, and each hot plate was on an automatic timer to switch it off at the end of the evening.[8] The lights were on throughout their home, and our hosts asked us to kindly remember not to flip them off, especially in the restroom, lest they be left in the dark at quite an inopportune moment. Like the food, bathroom lights were on automatic timers, set to turn off at the end of the night. At every turn, in every detail, someone had prepared to make rest—deep, thorough rest—possible. The degree to which there was nothing that had to be done for twenty-four hours was beyond any version of Sabbath I'd experienced, before or since.

I didn't return from that trip and automate the electricity in my own home, but I did begin to approach the day before Sabbath with greater intentionality. I began to look around me for ways to prepare now for rest tomorrow. I put things completely away instead of leaving them out. I made a list of what had to be done ahead so I wouldn't be so inclined to sneak a task in "really quick," only to find

---

[8] Shabbat takes place from sundown Friday evening through sundown Saturday evening. Many observers extend their rest from work to include details non-Jewish people may not be aware of, such as plugging in devices and flipping light switches. For example, apartment buildings in neighborhoods with large Jewish communities may have a Sabbath elevator, which stops on every floor, thereby relieving the rider from the work of button pushing.

I'd sunk into my computer for half an hour and my kids were waiting for me to reemerge. After a bit of experimenting and refining there was no doubt: Our family was experiencing a more life-giving way of moving through the week because we didn't just have a time for Sabbath marked off, we had practices to prepare for Sabbath's arrival.

After planning and preparing, think about what would be restful or fun for your family. Rather than making a plan to certainly do those things, let them be a springboard for everyone to decide what sounds good when the time comes. Maybe the final decision gets rotated among the members of your family, maybe you all agree together, or maybe you flip a coin. Likely, there will be some things that you find aren't restful after all and need to be ruled out from future Sabbaths.

Which brings us, finally, to the most important part of beginning this practice as a family: knowing and embracing that building a Family Sabbath takes some experimentation. Your family will need to try out a few different versions of this to figure out what works for you and what doesn't; what actually is restful for you all, and what just isn't, as much as it sounded good ahead of time.

Our family has practiced Sabbath together pretty regularly over the years, and I can attest to how it morphs along the way. When our kids were very young, we could plan for one day each week, because we only needed to account for my and my husband's schedules. Preparation looked mainly like tidying the house and responding to final emails the night before. And whatever specifically we decided to do, we *needed* to get out of the house. The monotony of babyhood inside the same four walls meant that staying in was anything but restful.

Now, with kids who are nine and seven, we've shifted to a two-part practice: We block as much of Saturday as we can for Sabbath (which we simply call "Family Day") and we also have a Sunday dinner, a new practice we added on, born from reflecting on the story of Deuteronomy, where Sabbath rhythms didn't just offer rest, but also helped provide for everyone in the community. Inspired by that vision, we made a list of local family-owned restaurants and decided to order takeout each week. We rest and feast as a family (because doing the dishes is my anti-rest) and we invest in our neighbors at the same time.

The key to Family Sabbath is to consider how, in very practical ways, you can spend a chunk of time together that feels as good as the God who commissioned it is. My answer and yours could look wildly different, but if we come to the end of the time more connected to the goodness of God and our identity as image-bearers, we're on the right track.

Now remember: This is your family's web. These are your strands to weave to give your web a shape all your own, which means these ideas are inspiration, a place to start. The last thing you should do is all of them (or at least, not all at once). Instead, focus on the goal: anchoring your child to a God who is good. So pick a practice to try that fits who your child is, what your family enjoys, and what fits in your real life. A young child might love finding life-giving words on a note in their lunch, while an older child might connect best with a family code word that means "You are loved," but sounds not-embarrassing-in-front-of-my-friends (ugh!).

CONSIDER

What are you already doing, individually or as a family, that helps you experience God's goodness? How could that be leaned into, tweaked, or expanded?

What sort of experiment can you try first in order to make anchoring in and experiencing the goodness of God part of your family's life?

May I also remind you: God's goodness is for you too. You are not tasked with teaching it to your kid; you are invited to experience it alongside them, out in the world God so lovingly made.

CHAPTER 6

God Is Powerful

When my son Riley was seven, he was having a particularly difficult time with nightmares. More often than not, he'd cry out at 2:00 a.m. in his youngest-sounding voice, and I'd scramble out of bed, knowing that if he spent too long in the dark with his fear he wouldn't be able to recover, and sleep would be lost for the night for both of us.

We'd perform our ritual of naming happy thoughts, then taking deep breaths while wiggling our toes. I'd repeat and repeat, "You are safe and loved. Yes, the dream was scary, and you are safe and loved." Then I'd pray for him.

I wanted to pray for God to take away bad dreams. I wanted to ask God for only happy dreams and good sleep. I wanted to pray bold and confident prayers for my son that showed what I truly believe about God in these moments: that God is near, eager to help, as concerned with the nightmares of a child at 2:00 a.m. as with any great problem of the world. I wanted Riley to hear God's whisper, "Do not fear. You are worth more than many sparrows" (see Matt. 10:31).

But I didn't. I couldn't, because I didn't believe the nightmares would stop. What if I prayed for the end of bad dreams and he had another one? Would that hurt his faith? Was asking for help the wrong kind of prayer?

My own web of faith is anchored to the God who is powerful, able to do anything. But the other end of that thread is the truth that God is wise, and knows what is best, in ways I do not. From the anchor point of God's wisdom, I picture another strand extending out like a V, anchoring to God's goodness. Then the triangle closes, reminding me of what Pastor Ben Patterson once told our gymnasium full of collegians during chapel: "Everything in prayer depends on who you think you're praying to. It's like a three-legged stool. There is God's power: Can God do what is best? God's wisdom: Does God really know what is best? And God's love: Does God care? Does God really want what is best? God's power, God's wisdom, and God's love," he would say, "are infinite. They are perfect."

The trio of power, love, and wisdom reminds us that while God's power is *an* anchor point, the thread is tethered to other true attributes as well, which together help us not only pray boldly, but also process what may or may not happen after prayer. This trio is one example of why our web of faith is anchored to many attributes of God, not just one. Growing in our trust for God often includes allowing our expectations for one trait to be informed by the others. God's ability to do things is also informed by God's deep wisdom about what should be done and deep love for those making the request. As our anchor threads connect various attributes together, we are better able to approach God without trying to *use* God.

Considered a slightly different way, think about how often we tell kids miracle stories as proof of God's power. We astonish them with the exodus and wow them with the story of Jesus walking on the sea. The stories are indeed amazing, and cultivating amazement is a great thing to do with our kids. But sometimes we stop at amazement when we could move on to what that amazement is supposed to lead us to: meaning.

Every miracle God did has both a what and a why. The what of the exodus includes plagues and the parting of the sea, a pillar of cloud and fire, and manna in the desert. Amazing. It's a miracle-extravaganza for Israel. But each one of those miracles points to deeper truths about both God's identity and Israel's:

- **Plagues** don't just show power, they show Yahweh God's unique power that extends even over the gods of Egypt. You have a river god? Watch what Yahweh can do to the Nile!

- **Parting the sea** doesn't just usher the people to freedom, it calls back to the creation story, where God's Spirit hovers over the waters. God had power over the waters then, and still does. Waters, by the way, were a symbol of chaos in the ancient Near East, something that makes complete sense if you've ever been helplessly tossed about by a particularly giant wave. So, when we see God having authority over water, it points to God's ability to create order and goodness, even over the most unruly areas of creation. (Which is good, because I know my own personal area of creation tends toward the unruly at times.)

- **Providing manna and quail** doesn't just fill Israelites' bellies, it helps them learn to trust God alone to provide for them. Yahweh is a God of life and abundance, even in the wilderness.

God's power is not just generic strength. It's not the ability to do tricks that wow us, like a caped magician on a stage. God's power also reveals something of God's character: God is not like the gods of the nations, confined to one small territory and impotent in the faraway land of Egypt. Instead, God is great everywhere. Amid the chaos of nature and the chaos caused by people, God brings order, showing us something of God's goodness as well. God uses Their power to feed and care for the people, the exact opposite of the gods all around who expect to be cared for by the people.

The same is true when we turn to the story of Jesus walking on water. There's the what of the miracle, showing power over the chaotic and frightening sea (again). But the what points to the why: This Jesus possesses the same power as Yahweh God, Creator of all things, who tames the waters—of the deep, of the Red Sea, and now of the Sea of Galilee. When Jesus comforts his frightened friends by calling out "It is I," the words he uses, *ego eimi*, are exactly the same as in the Greek version of the book of Exodus, when God speaks God's own name, "I AM, Yahweh." Jesus isn't just showing his power over nature, but his power over all.

Helping our kids anchor to a God who is powerful is about moving with them from the wow to the who and the why. That is, what does God's power show us about God's character, purposes for the world, and invitation for humanity? The wow is terrific, and for kids it's often really fun as well. But if we stop at wow, it only makes sense that misconceptions about God and God's power take root.

First, God may become a genie (and prayer is the way we rub the lamp). Kids will come to see the purpose of God's power as happiness insurance and crisis prevention. The purpose of knowing the powerful God is to access God when you need help. You'll recall that therapeutic deism imagines a far-off god whose purpose is primarily to make our lives better, happier, more comfortable, or less tragic. When our conversations with kids about God's power stop at wow, we play into this particular misunderstanding of God.

Similarly, talking about God's power in isolation can create a sense that God is a superhero, whose power is for the purpose of intervention. Superheroes are good precisely because they intervene in affairs to protect someone. It isn't only something they are able to do, it's something they must do, and often we find ourselves expecting the same of God. If God is powerful, God must use that power for good. Our expectations for the purposes of God's power are shaped less by stories from Scripture and more by Spider-Man's uncle Ben, who says, "With great power comes great responsibility."

CONSIDER

In what ways have you experienced genie-god or superhero-god, either personally or related to kids?

It's not hard to see how a genie-god or superhero-god is bound to let a child down. As life's inevitable hurts and hardships come, they'll expect God's help in the form of miraculous intervention, like the stories they've been wowed by. While there are certainly times God does intervene in our situations, perhaps more common is the experience of God's presence in the midst of hardship. We find ourselves strengthened, encouraged, and comforted, not by the change in our circumstances but by the presence of the Spirit of God. What's more, this often happens in ways that don't even make sense to us, especially in light of the situation. We find that there really can be peace that goes beyond understanding. If a child hasn't had the chance to move from being wowed by power to connecting with the person, it will be much harder for them to experience that peace.

But if, instead, we put God's power in its proper context, we might find that it can be a comfort to realize God's power is not for flash or show. That it's amazing, but not for our amazement alone. In our wonder, we're invited to ask why. Why this display of power? Why this act? What does it show us about God?

Knowing that every miracle has a why, we can approach miracle stories with kids ready to cultivate curiosity and wonder. In fact, the specific tool of "wonder questions" helps draw out the layers of a miracle. It sounds like this in the story of one of my favorite of Jesus' miracles:

Feeding the Crowd

One time, Jesus was sitting on a hillside with his disciples when a large crowd came to find him. Crowds had a way of finding Jesus. Some people came to hear what he would say about God, while others came to see if he would do something special, like heal someone. In one book of the Bible, John, these special actions are called "signs," which reminds us that they were done to point to an important, true thing about who God is or what God was up to.

This was one of those times that Jesus was, indeed, going to perform a sign for the people. See if you can figure out what this sign points to.

Jesus asked one disciple, named Philip, "Where shall we buy bread for these people to eat?" and you can tell from his answer how this question made Philip feel: "Even if we could find a breadmaker, it would cost us half the money we make in a year to buy all the bread they had, which wouldn't be anywhere near enough. Everyone would get one bite." Philip was overwhelmed by how impossible the answer to the question was. Then Andrew, another disciple, jumped in and said, "Here's a boy with five little rolls of bread and two fish." Imagine the group looking at the small lunch. It wouldn't be enough to share with even one other person, let alone a huge group of thousands.

I wonder how long this conversation went on.

I wonder what Jesus expected the disciples to do after he asked that question. I wonder if he expected anything specific from them at all.

Here's what happened next. Jesus told the disciples, "Have the people sit down." People found spots on the grassy hillside overlooking the glittering lake. And Jesus took the loaves, gave thanks, and started passing out bread bits to the group. He took the fish, gave thanks, and started passing out fish chunks to the group. And the Bible says people could have as much as they wanted. They ate and ate until they were completely full.

Bread and fish are fine foods, of course, but let's imagine you were the boy, and you had picked your favorite lunch to bring along. What would you want to see Jesus multiply for this meal?

Back to the hillside. For people living when Jesus lived, food didn't come from stores full of choices. Food was grown and made by hand, and there wasn't always enough. So this meal would have been special for so many reasons: It was a surprise feast, it was all you could eat, and of course, it was made by a miracle.

I wonder what the people thought and felt as they returned home that night.

I wonder if they understood what this sign of bread for all pointed to about who God is or what God was doing.

We don't need to look hard for an answer to that last question. The story goes on the very next day. Jesus was in a new location, not too far from the one the day before, but somewhere far enough away that the people needed to look for him. And look they did, until they found him again.

They were back in hopes of more bread, more fish. Jesus said to them, "You came to find me not because you understood the sign but because you filled up on the bread I gave you. You just want more to eat!"

And as the people asked questions, and as Jesus kept talking with them, they remembered another time God had fed a huge group: long ago when there was manna in the desert. "Moses gave us bread from heaven!" they said. "What will you give us?" But Jesus took the chance to make something clearer to them: "God gave you bread from heaven. And God gave you me. I'm bread from heaven."

This made the crowd think, *Um, Jesus, you're not bread and you're not from heaven. We know your mom and dad. You're from Nazareth.* But Jesus was hoping they'd see what the sign pointed to.

Do you have a guess?

Jesus was there to give the people life. Just like literal bread feeds us and gives us life, Jesus came to give us life. The people were hungry again, but Jesus was offering himself. They liked the food, but Jesus was offering friendship.

GOD'S POWER AS INVITATION

As we talked about above, a miracle story like this one from John 6 is an opportunity for us to move beyond amazement to a deeper understanding of the connections between God's power and God's character and purposes.

On the hill in John 6, Jesus is surrounded by a crowd who, we're told, had followed him because they saw the signs he was doing. John always calls miracles "signs," which I find abundantly helpful, because it's a clue to what he believes we should think of miracles. They point to something.

Often, with children, we present the signs in a circular fashion: Jesus uses power to perform a miracle; that miracle is a sign; the sign points to how powerful Jesus is. In John, we find something quite different. He invites us to look from the power of the miracle toward something more deeply significant about Jesus.

YOUR KID ASKS

How come God doesn't do miracles now?

Consider that the best approach is to ask back, "How do you know God doesn't?" Help your child consider the ways that God's presence, care, and leading might not be grand but are nevertheless real. Don't start by coming to God's defense and trying to convince your child miracles happen. Instead, help them hold space for the possibility that miracles could happen, based on who God is.

Jesus himself tells us what the sign of multiplying bread and fish was supposed to point toward: the truth that Jesus is the Bread of Life. He is offering the people nothing more and nothing less than himself, and that all who draw near to him will find life in abundance. As is often the case with God's power, the purpose of using it was to call people into a growing, life-sustaining relationship.

And then Andrew brings a boy to Jesus, and Jesus chooses to start with that small offering. The miracle would have wowed us just as much if Jesus had just *poof!* made food appear from nowhere. But then it wouldn't have told us as much about the character of God, and how God chooses to use Their power. Jesus chooses to use his power in partnership with the boy. As I've noted already, this has been God's hope from the beginning—to partner with humanity to create a world that is fruitful and multiplies. Here Jesus is partnering with Andrew and the boy by choice so that food will multiply out to the hungry crowd. Life and abundance, spreading far and wide.

And yet, this is not about Andrew. And it's not about the boy. Their participation is certainly important, but the reason it's important is how it points back to Jesus' purposes in partnering with people.

I've heard so many children's lessons about the boy, about how he obediently gave Jesus what he had, about how kids should be like the boy and bring everything they have to Jesus. The worst thing that happens to this story is that it becomes all about how the boy shared. Nothing turns such a deep story into a shallow one like "Now, child, go and share likewise." Because now, what we've taught kids is not that our powerful God wants to work alongside us to bring life and abundance into the world, but that Jesus sounds just like their teachers and parents and coaches, wanting them to share more.

Beyond that, focusing on the boy's actions as a model to copy implies Jesus did the miracle *because* the boy shared, putting us just a short hop away from being the ones who control God's power through our right course of action. When it comes to sharing his lunch, I wonder if the boy had much choice in the matter, given the role children played in the culture. I wonder if Andrew even asked him if he wanted to be part of what was going on, or if he just assumed a rabbi could take a lunch from a kid. Did the boy worry that he was about to be hungry? We know little about the particulars of his involvement, certainly not enough to build this child up as a model of obedience for other children to copy. He was there, with what he had, and however he came to be giving his lunch away to Jesus, because it was Jesus, goodness was as abundant as the meal.

When we limit the purposes of God's power to impressing us or fixing our in-the-moment problems, we are likely to miss where the power points. The crowd certainly did. They find Jesus again the following day, and why have they returned? They hope for more bread. Yet, as Jesus turns from the power to feed them to the purpose of feeding them, and says that he's bread, they complain.

And if we're honest, so do we.

All too often, we expect God to use Their power in accordance with our purposes, and then we fault God if that doesn't happen. We get stuck in how God's power can provide for us in a situation, without also considering how God's presence can carry us through a situation, even one that doesn't change, that fails to improve.

We are like the people in the story, who try one more time to get Jesus to make bread by calling back the story of manna in the wilderness. God gave them bread. You claim you are from God. You can give us bread…again. But that story, of manna in the wilderness, wasn't actually about bread either. In fact, it aligns pretty nicely with our main point here: God's power is often used for the purpose of relationship. In the desert, God was inviting the newly freed people to experience God as trustworthy and caring, in order that they would respond with trust themselves. The hope was for them to become a people who exclusively trusted God to care for them, and didn't turn to the gods of the nations to see if those gods might do the job better.

SPIRAL THE STORY

In addition to focusing on God's power, here are some ideas for spiraling back to the story of feeding the crowd with a God-centered storytelling approach:

- God partners with people. As with creation, this is a story that shows God's choice to partner as Jesus turns to the disciples and invites them in, and begins the miracle with the boy's lunch. The people weren't heroes who saved the day; they were just regular people included in what Jesus did.

- God cares for us. The people were hungry, and it mattered to Jesus that they were fed. This is one story that helps kids see that all our needs are important to God.

- God is a life-giver. Jesus calls himself the bread of life, an image of nourishment that points to how God wants us, and everyone else, to have life. With kids, it can help to note that this is about both literally being alive and also quality of life.

From the very beginning, what God offered us was God Themself. God's hope was, and is, for us to really live connected to God, enjoying God's presence, experiencing God's peace. God's power was a tool by which we could grow in trusting God. The power demonstrated in creation culminates in wanting a relationship with humanity. The power demonstrated in the exodus culminates in wanting a relationship with Israel. The power demonstrated on the hillside culminates in wanting a relationship with the people who have returned for bread.

The power invites us to know the person.

And, like the crowd, many people find that quite disappointing. There is a sense of: That's it? A mighty God who could do so much for me is focused most on offering Their own self?

The crowd wants to live contractually: Our obedience in exchange for your power. Send manna, we'll obey. (They didn't.)

Give bread, we'll obey. (They don't.) Wow us, we'll obey. (We won't.) The obedience contract breaks down quickly, because God does not use God's power for the purpose of wowing us. God uses power to move the world closer to God's dream. In this case, the dream that people would trust Jesus, exclusively, to protect and provide for them, just as God dreamed Israel would trust God, exclusively, to protect and provide for them in the wilderness.

The power-obedience contract doesn't work, but the signs instead point from power → person → trust.

All this brings us back to prayer, to how and why we come to God. Instead of seeing it as the way we access power, the summons to a superhero, like a Jesus-shaped bat signal, we see it as the way we grow connection with the person that power points us toward.

PRAYING TO BUILD RELATIONSHIP

As you help your child practice connecting to God through prayer, use images that focus on cultivating a relationship. When prayer is presented as growing a friendship and enjoying time together, that allows a kid to still talk about the things they and others need without reducing prayer to a mechanism by which you access fix-it power.

If I'm inviting a group of kids to pray with me, I'll often say, "Let's pray together. Prayer is just talking with God using our regular words about the regular things we are thinking and feeling, because, like any good friend, God loves to hear from us." If we're listening for God together, I'll say, "Let's pray together. Because prayer is like talking with a friend, and today we're going to be the listeners in the conversation. Listening to God takes practice, since we don't hear God like you hear me. Here's what we're going to do…"

Kids need not only time and practice with prayer but also options for the form prayer takes. I remember asking my mom if I really *had* to fold my hands, bow my head, and close my eyes. And what would happen if I opened my eyes? She readily assured me that those were simply directions to help us listen, and that it was indeed okay not to do them, so long as we didn't instead talk loudly or otherwise distract people who were praying with us. From then on, I often peeked, though that never yielded anything more interesting than the occasional eye contact with a fellow peeker.

How might kids pray beyond calm stillness? Here are some ideas to get started:

Category Prayers

Start here: Give your child a category to pray for and take turns naming something that fits in. You might say, "Let's take turns thanking God for things in nature! I'll name something, then you name something, and we'll see how many we can think of." When the list winds down, offer a simple closing, "God, You've made an amazing world. Thank You! Amen."

While you may nominate a category like people you love or activities you do for fun, this can also work for topics like things that are hard right now, things that make us scared or worried, or people we know who are sad or struggling.

Age it up: With older children, you can adjust your introduction away from sounding like you're launching a game and instead simply say, "I thought this time as we prayed we could notice the good things God's given us in our home." They will also be able to nominate categories as they get older, which you could invite by saying something like, "We're going to pray for people this time. Who do you think we should start with? Family and friends? Or people from some part of the world or who have a particular experience? You pick."

Breath Prayers

A breath prayer is as simple as something you say as you breathe in, and something you say as you breathe out. The sentence can be anything, and can be said anywhere, anytime.

Breath prayer can be a great way to pray at bedtime to encourage resting in love. It can be a great way to help a child pray at school, where you help them pick a phrase ahead of time that they can use. Its portability can make it especially accessible for kids.

Start here: Give your kid some short phrases to try, such as:

- Inhale: You are with me. Exhale: I am not alone.
- Inhale: I am your child. Exhale: I am always loved.
- Inhale: You love me. Exhale: No matter what.

Age it up: Invite kids to create their own breath prayer. Perhaps there is an attribute of God that feels important for them to remember. Or, maybe there's a verse or Bible story they like that can be a jumping-off point.

Moving Prayers

Moving prayers invite kids to use their whole bodies as they connect with God.

Start here: Take the category-style prayer I mentioned previously, only crouch down low until an idea comes, then jump up high to name it out.

Dot Prayers

Place five different-colored dots on the walls with a note card or draw them on the ground with chalk. Call out a color and a fun way to move. Once your child arrives at the dot, call out a prayer prompt. Then repeat.

The prompts could all be thematic, such as "praying for people," where each shape is a different group: a family member, a classmate or teammate, a friend, people around the world, or yourself. The theme "emotions" could be focused on sharing with God something that makes you feel sad, happy, nervous, excited, or thankful.

Prayer Postures

- Reach up: What is something we love about God?
- Reach out: What is something happening in our world that we want God to help with?
- Hold hands: Who is someone we know that we want to pray for?
- Hands to heart: What do you want to say to God or ask God about today?

Art as Prayer

Prayers don't need to be verbal to be authentic. Why not grab paper and colors, or sidewalk chalk, put on some music, and draw a prayer?

You could give a prompt for the picture, such as:

- Let's draw the people we want to pray for today.
- Let's draw a time we felt sad or scared and ask God to help us if something similar happens again.

- Let's draw something we love to do and thank God for it.

However, this can also work if you say, "Let's color with God. Although we don't see or hear God in the same way you see or hear me, God is here, so let's make some pictures together."

Praying in ways that help us connect to God relationally removes the pressure to use just the right words in just the right order, asking for just the right things to access the help of genie-god. It helps us anchor to a God who is both powerful and present, a God who can do anything but who also is perfectly wise and loving about what and when to do so. It removes the false expectations of a quick fix by superhero-god, and replaces them with the rich presence of the God who enters in, suffers with, carries through. The power is for the purpose of connecting us to the person so that we, and our kids, find the real God offering God's own self to us in the midst of any circumstance.

CONSIDER

What are you already doing, individually or as a family, that helps you experience God's power as an invitation to God's presence? How could that be leaned into, tweaked, or expanded?

Ultimately, this is how I prayed for Riley in that stretch: "God, we know You care that Riley is having bad dreams, and we are asking You to help. We want You to give him good sleep, with only good dreams. But even if they happen again, help him know You are here and he is not alone. Help him know You are bigger than the scary dreams, that You are with him and You love him. Amen." I prayed for him about dreams, like Paul once prayed for us: to know how high and wide and long and deep is the love of God (see Eph. 3:18). Perhaps that would happen by the power of God changing the situation, or perhaps it would happen by God offering God's presence to a seven-year-old and his mama, exhausted and afraid in the middle of the night.

CHAPTER 7

God Is Just

The three rectangular tables in the conference room were set up to form a sort of horseshoe shape with a whiteboard standing off in one corner. On two of the three sides sat members of a church-wide strategy team, while our children's ministry leadership was shoulder to shoulder on side three, effectively ensuring that wherever I looked I'd see either confusion or that face someone makes when they already know what they think and are just trying to figure out how to tell you how it's going to be.

For their part, the strategy team had been tasked with considering how each ministry department best fit in with the future goals of the church. Meanwhile, our team had worked for weeks on language to try to communicate why our approach—God-centered storytelling, exploration instead of dictated application, live teachers instead of video curriculum—was both wise and effective. We hoped to both educate and convince this group of what we had been seeing for the past few years: This approach worked better than what we'd been doing previously—polishing moralistic content into a hyper-entertaining, high-sheen package.

It wasn't going well.

The feedback was ho-hum, and finally one member, a man in his mid-thirties with nephews in our program, leaned back in his chair and said, "I dunno, it just seems like it doesn't matter all *that* much what kids learn. I just want them to have, like, a basic foundation. They just need to know God loves them and have fun while they're there. Anything else will come when they get to middle school or high school."

He'd said the quiet part out loud, this colleague of ours. This church mainly just wanted to be sure that when a kid was picked up at the end of the service, they'd had fun. They wanted kids to "drag their parents to church" because of the whiz-bang activities that happened there. (Once, while we were trying to educate the church's leadership about the unique role of faith cheerleaders, and how cultivating those relationships could both increase retention and serve families well, we were asked to instead fly out a Disney star for a visit.)

Now, I am neither anti-Disney nor anti-fun, not by a long shot. Fun is vital, a goal we shared with this ad hoc committee. But they wanted a main dish of fun with a side of "God loves you," whereas we wanted fun to be a tool that helped a kid feel safe and connected enough to do what really mattered: Connect with God. Not just know they were loved by God, but know God. Not just hear a story about God, but practice spending time with God.

The rest of the content of that meeting isn't terribly relevant here, unless some of you are wondering if your best family faith strategy involves Disney celebrities. But the core idea that all a kid needs is to know that God is love and God loves them is pervasive. It's also wrongheaded. Well-meaning adults think that's all kids need, but it's not, because the world has gone wrong, and kids know it.

In ways big and small, kids experience sin and its effects. Often they are more sensitive to it than adults. They don't always have the language to describe or interpret what they observe about sin, but they are aware of what I often categorize in kid-speak as "hard and sad" things happening near and far. As adults, we might use the word *injustice* instead.

Since kids are aware of what is wrong in the world—they see injustice—they wonder if God is going to make it right—to bring justice. Does God see? Does God care? Most of all: What is God going to do about it? Lo and behold, we find the story of Scripture full of both these types of questions and resounding answers: Yes, God sees. Yes, God cares. And, to be precise, God plans to remake the world such that it works the way it was meant to, which is to say, abundantly good, full of justice. I will sometimes describe God's dream to children as "all good and no bad, all joy and no sad. It's where everyone knows they are unconditionally loved, and they treat others well because they know they are too."

And the Bible? How does *it* describe all this? Let's consider just four examples, two from the Old Testament and two from the New Testament, that are emblematic of the narrative arc related to justice in Scripture. What we find is that God is consistently concerned with people experiencing justice and equity. When the world gets off track, God works to bring it back on track again.

If you were to read the whole story of Leviticus (and despite appearances, there *is* a story in there), here's what you'd find. Israel is shaped, most of all, by the story of the exodus, of being the ones God freed from slavery, led by God through the sea and across the desert. So how shall they now live as God's people, together?

Here's a peek:

Consecrate the fiftieth year and proclaim liberty throughout the land to all its inhabitants. It shall be a jubilee for you; each of you is to return to your family property and to your own clan. (Leviticus 25:10 NIV)

This fiftieth year is called Jubilee, and it's like a super Sabbath, with feasting and rest for land, animals, and people. Significantly, each parcel of land reverts back to its original owners who might have, in the interim, fallen on hard times and needed to sell it and go to work for another landowner. Jubilee is the idea that while there will inevitably be some who prosper and some who don't in the short term—often because of their own good or bad choices but sometimes because of bad luck, or health, or whatever other factors—these differences in outcomes should not lead to permanent inequality. Every fifty years a family is given a new start; the playing field is releveled. The means of supporting one's family is restored, equally, rather than wealth being steadily concentrated in the hands of a few. There are not some who have to work three minimum-wage jobs to support their family while others fly themselves to space on…um…*suggestively* shaped rockets, shall we say. If only Leviticus were relevant to life today…

It's as simple as this: Our God is an Exodus God, so we will be Jubilee people. God goes first to rescue us; we respond by being restorers for one another.

Let's turn to a second example, one that helps us with the misconception of God's justice as a punishment God administers to wrongdoers, whether that's in the present or at the end of the age. A passage like Hosea 5:10 shows why that idea persists:

> *Judah's leaders are like those who move boundary stones. I will pour out my wrath on them like a flood of water.* (NIV)

On the surface, God may seem arbitrarily angry. But reading just a bit deeper reveals crucial context for the passage and insight into the nature of God's justice.

What are boundary stones, and why is God so persnickety about those who move them? As Israel settles into the Promised Land, there is a fundamental right of each family in the nation to have their own land, one we've already seen protected through the practice of Jubilee. In the economic context of the day, this was their means of production, their way to support a family and make a living.

Boundary stones mark, you guessed it, the boundaries of one family's land in a context where you can't just go to city hall and get the assessor's office maps of the property lines.

Here's the key: It isn't the poor or powerless who move a boundary marker to try to expand what belongs to them; it's the powerful who think they can get away with it.

Moving a boundary marker is emblematic of the way wealth and power usually work, where they are used to get more, to build an empire that promises, like all idols do, to protect and provide for the one who moves the marker. Deuteronomy, and the rest of the Old Testament, however, show us an expectation that equity should be valued over empire. God is not arbitrarily angry that someone moved a rock. God is rightly angry that the powerful misused their power at the expense of the powerless and figured no one could stop them.

Jumping ahead to Jesus' arrival, we read about a time when he stood in front of his community to clarify his purposes. Luke 4: 17–19 tells us that

> *the scroll of Isaiah the prophet was handed to him. He unrolled the scroll and found the place where this was written:*
> *"The Spirit of the LORD is upon me, for he has anointed me to bring Good News to the poor. He has sent me to proclaim that captives will be released, that the blind will see, that the oppressed will be set free, and that the time of the LORD's favor has come." (NIV)*

That final phrase, "the time of the LORD's favor," is a reference to Jubilee. Of all the images Jesus could have drawn upon to help people understand what animated his mission, he chose the most radical reorientation of economics that the community knew.

The news Jesus had for the people was good because it changed the lived reality of the poor and the marginalized. This was not different from Jesus' work against sin; it was an example of it. Sin's effects include the misuse and abuse of power, the sidelining of the powerless, and injustice, which inevitably results in people suffering. But the God who is just had already set forth a vision for release and restoration—Jubilee—which Jesus was taking to the next level.

Fourth and finally, there's the line Jesus offers us in the Lord's

Prayer: "Your kingdom come, your will be done, on earth as it is in heaven" (Matt. 6:10 NIV). This isn't a saccharine-sweet prayer for peace on earth, an after-school special asking, "Can't we all just get along?" This is a prayer for a radical reworking of the status quo, such that anything that is out of alignment with God's own character would no longer be "just how things work around here."

An earth that matches heaven would be just, because God is just. God longs for the world to work in ways that are fair, honoring, and equitable for the people God made and loves. God cares that the world as we know it today *actually* works in ways that are unfair, dishonoring, and inequitable for so many people, especially those with less power or fewer resources.

YOUR KID ASKS

Why doesn't God just fix it?

This question is a great example of the tensions we hold when we are getting to know God in God's complicated mystery. So you might say, "Yes, God is just, and God will fix it. But the way God fixes things is with people, so we need to help. And someday injustice will end forever."

God's justice and goodness are connected, the latter expressed through the former. For the biblical writers, there is a strong sensibility that in order for God to be good, God must bring an end to the bad, a perspective shaped by experiences of oppression. Allan Boesak, a Black South African theologian, reminds us that "people who do not know oppression and suffering react strangely to the language of the Bible. The truth is that God is the God of the poor and the oppressed. Because they are powerless, God will take up their cause…The oppressed do not see any dichotomy between God's love and God's justice."

When we help kids anchor to a God who is just, we are offering them assurance that God's posture toward evil is not passive observation, but engaging to set wrong things right. To say that God will win and evil will lose is also to say that justice will win and oppression will lose.

One story that can bring this to light for kids? The time Jesus got big mad.

It was almost Passover, an important holiday for God's people. Passover was a time to remember how God had freed them from slavery in Egypt. Jesus was in Jerusalem, the capital city, which was also where the temple was. The temple was an important building for God's people. It was a place to worship God, to talk about Scripture together, and to be together with other Jewish people.

These two things combined—an important holiday and an important place—meant that lots of people had come to Jerusalem, some from quite far away.

Part of worship at the time included bringing something to give to God, an offering. The type of offering a family brought depended on whether they had a lot or a little. Richer families brought certain types of offerings; poorer families had different types of gifts that were more affordable for them.

On a long trip to Jerusalem, it often wasn't possible to bring the offering along, but that was okay! Once you arrived, there were money changers at the temple—people who could exchange money for the offering.

That sounds like a great plan, right? Well, it would be, if the money changers didn't also charge extra. It could be, if that extra charge wasn't especially hard on poorer families. But they did charge extra, and it was especially hard on people who were poor. Worship had become a business, and an unjust one at that.

Here's the question: What do you think God thought of this? How do you imagine God felt about this? Why?

Here's how Matthew tells it: "And Jesus entered the temple and drove out all those who were buying and selling in the temple, and overturned the tables of the money changers and the seats of those who were selling [the offerings for those who were poorer]. And He said to them, 'It is written: "My house shall be called a house of prayer"; but you are making it a robbers' den'" (Matt. 21:12–13 NASB).

Jesus was mad. Very mad. And being mad was the exact right way to be, about the exact right issue: injustice, especially injustice done by people who said they loved and trusted God.

What's important—critical—about Jesus' anger was the source. He was mad about something God *should* be mad about. It's important for God to have a deep, emotional reaction to injustice; the alternative implies God accepts it. Shrugs it off as inevitable. Despite how often we see people claiming God actually sides with the powerful, even if they use that power in abhorrent ways, the biblical story says that God's answer comes from God's justice.

Perhaps you were introduced to God's anger in a way that simply left you afraid of it. This might be the case, for instance, if you were told rather indiscriminately that sin makes God mad. When we have the chance to consider *what about sin* might make God mad, and to look through the story of Scripture for an answer, we find a clear, resounding theme: Injustice. Oppression. The hoarding of power by some at the expense of others. The biblical vision of God's people, beginning early in Old Testament law, and carrying on to the New Testament church, was one where anyone with an abundance would allow it to overflow to the marginalized, until there were no margins.

This gives us the lens with which to see Jesus' actions at the temple. He specifically rebukes the vendors who sell doves, the offering of the poor. While the entire enterprise of profiting off worship practices angers him, his most potent words focus on oppressing the poor. It's the powerful who overcharge a family for their doves, because they can get away with it. He isn't generically mad at the money changers; he is specifically mad at the injustice that has seeped into the worship system and poisoned it.

SPIRAL THE ATTRIBUTE

In addition to the story of clearing the temple courts, here are some ideas for spiraling back to God's justice in other parts of the Bible:

- Make it a fun fact. Say to your child: Did you know the Bible talks about God's justice hundreds of times? I wonder why it comes up so much.
- Explore Zacchaeus's response to Jesus. The choice

to not only repay but to repay four times above what was taken shows that Zacchaeus recognized, as someone with power and money, that restorative justice was the next right step after encountering Jesus (see Luke 19:8).

- Gentle words, strong words. Talk together about times Jesus used gentle words with people: Who was he speaking to? Were they powerful or not? What about when Jesus used strong words? Help your child notice the ways Jesus was pointing to a more just community in the way he spoke.

Here are some ways we might invite our kids to anchor to a God who is just.

STAY THE COURSE

One hot Wednesday afternoon in the summer of 2020, my sons and I drove west on the 10 freeway, watching the Los Angeles skyline grow taller as the minutes passed. In the trunk was a bag with seven types of snacks atop a trio of neon posters declaring "Black Lives Matter." A colleague from my time at the Christian college had gone on to help lead the Los Angeles chapter of Black Lives Matter while continuing as a faculty member in Christian higher education. She was one of a few Black coworkers who graciously and patiently helped me learn about systemic racism, power, and privilege. Most of all, she helped me understand how all the unlearning and relearning I was doing was not a justice-focused form of moralism, the right thing to do in some abstract sense. This was spiritual formation.

When I saw her post online about the first in-person collective action to be taken since the pandemic, in response to the murder of George Floyd, I realized that this was also a chance to invite my kids into the spiritual practice of bearing witness to injustice.

I parked in the Los Angeles Cathedral's garage, and my boys and I made our way down the hill to the Department of Justice. We stood near the back, where they had a little more wiggle room, and listened. They made their way through all seven different snacks. And when the heat and grown-upness of it all took its toll on them, we hiked back up the hill to the car.

On the car rides, we talked about bearing God's image, about rightly using power, about giving our time and presence to things that matter to God. We talked about how this one event alone would not solve things, but that didn't mean it was useless to attend.

A lot of white families like mine went to a demonstration in the summer of 2020. A lot of white families didn't do much after that. I wonder if we faded away in part because we failed to see that practicing anti-racism is a form of discipleship, part of becoming like Jesus, who flipped the tables. Inviting our kids to participate in the process of seeking a more equitable society helps them anchor to a God who is just. Perhaps we resist because we know too much about the slowness of justice, the resistance to justice, and the reaction against justice-seeking. But even that connects us to the story of Scripture, because it's the same sensibility captured by the words of the psalmist:

How long, O LORD? How long will the wicked be allowed to gloat?

How long will they speak with arrogance? How long will these evil people boast?

They crush your people, LORD, hurting those you claim as your own.

They kill widows and foreigners and murder orphans.

"The LORD isn't looking," they say, "and besides, the God of Israel doesn't care." (Psalm 94:3–7 NLT)

Notably, it is back to God that the psalmist goes with their complaint that a just God is not doing enough quickly enough about injustice. It is not new to feel the tension between a just God and an unjust world, between a powerful God who shares and self-limits Their power, between a loving God and the fact that love doesn't control, but we'd like to see things controlled sometimes. We are right with the biblical writers as we hold all those things at once.

To put the form this work might take into bullet points risks insulting those who specialize in leading us forward, so I hope you are also reading those whose work focuses on raising kids to understand and work against racism and other forms of marginalization and injustice. But as you discern the form this takes for your family, may I offer some traits that we share as we anchor to God's justice in this way?

- It's ongoing. I write as a white mom, who could pop in and out of this work largely unaffected. But the reality that God's justice isn't a project but a characteristic of God calls me to an ongoing commitment to racial justice in my context.
- It's personal. When God is angry at injustice, it's because

people God loves are suffering. When a boundary stone is moved, the people whose land is taken are hurt, and the people, the beloved, made-in-God's-own-image people drive the call to seek justice.

- It's systemic. It'd be easy for the money changers at the temple to react defensively to Jesus: "Hey, man, I know this isn't a great system here, but that's just the way things are." Falling back on "the way things are" keeps systems and structures humming along that need to be disrupted and fully reimagined. Loving my neighbor means caring if the way things are done impacts my neighbor in an unjust way.

TALKING OPENLY

Three large, freestanding blue fabric pinboards, each with carefully prepared visuals, stood at the edges of our space for fourth through sixth graders. The stage closed the square, and the kids sat on the floor in the middle of the displays. We were in a series on the fruit of the Spirit, talking specifically about peace. Usually with children the focus is peace in contrast to worry. This time, we were going to talk about peace in contrast to violence.

At each board an adult gave the kids a short and careful but accurate introduction to an injustice issue in the world. Kids were invited to ask questions and then given a way to pray about what they'd just learned. They put dots on a map to pray for places experiencing war. After learning about enslavement through bonded labor, they planted seeds in small planter beds under a sign quoting

James 3:18: "Those who are peacemakers will plant seeds of peace and reap a harvest of righteousness" (NLT).

While two stations engaged with global issues that impacted children, it was the third station that I was most passionate about, and most nervous about the experience going well. After all, I didn't know of any other white-cultured suburban church who brought in a social worker from the county to talk about domestic violence. The rules of church culture usually dictate that we ignore statistics and pretend every family is just fine, thank you very much. With wisdom and expertise, the social worker told our kids how safe families should feel and act, and gave language to what abuse might sound, feel, and look like. She told them the truth: God wants peace in your home, God wants you to be safe and loved all the time, God cares if a grown-up who should be safe is treating you the wrong way. Kids were invited to write or draw prayers on pieces of blue paper they taped onto a river poster below the words of Amos 5:24: "But let justice roll on like a river, righteousness like a never-failing stream!" (NIV).

Two significant things happened that Sunday: Some children were able to tell that social worker what was happening in their homes, and she took steps immediately to help them. And all the children experienced that the people of God turn toward the hard things in the world; we don't hide from them. The practice of talking about the hard things of the world shows that we trust a God who is just, who isn't far away ignoring suffering, or worse, who caused the suffering because the victims deserved it. God is deeply concerned about injustice in the world, and eager for the people of God to pray and act so that it would be made right.

When we fail to intentionally introduce kids to a God who is just, focusing exclusively on God's love and kindness, we set kids up for confusion as they encounter the more difficult experiences in our world. Whether they come to learn about these hardships through their peers, major events in the news, or personal experience, the reality is that as kids grow, they will learn that a lot of the world works in ways that are deeply misaligned with God's hopes.

We may find that we want to hide these things from our kids in an effort to protect them from the pain. Certainly we must consider their age, development, and temperament to know both when and how to talk about injustice in the world. But once we've done that, we may still find ourselves wary of wading into these topics because we know they'll ask, "Why doesn't God stop that from happening?" So we want to help God a bit with the PR on the whole "the world keeps suffering" thing by avoiding the topic for as long as we can.

Interestingly, the biblical authors spend far less time wondering why the world is full of hardship than we do. Their perspective seems to assume the world works this way, leaving them to ask, "What can we expect from Yahweh God *given* that this is how the world works?" and their answer seems to be "We can expect Yahweh God to do justice because God is just." And if Yahweh God is not bringing justice to the oppressed, we can speak up and tell God to get a move on, already, like Psalm 94 does.

What this means for us as parents is that instead of sheltering our kids from the hard things of the world, we can have a regular practice of talking about them in age-appropriate ways. This gives us the chance to remind kids of key truths: No evil is greater than God's justice, God cares about what is wrong, and part of how

God's justice happens is that people who love God work for it. It gives them a chance to pray for justice, because prayer is part of the work too.

A ONE-QUESTION RITUAL

My older son is coming to the end of the fourth grade, when state history is included in the curriculum. For us, that means a long unit learning about the missionization of California by the Spanish from 1769 to 1833. Depending on who gets to tell the story, this either had the effect of introducing modern agriculture to the indigenous communities and offering us beautiful Spanish-style complexes that can now be toured and make great wedding venues, or it had the effect of decimating more than 65 percent of the indigenous population and representing a false god of conquest and colonization to this day.

Depending on who gets to tell the story.

When the fourth graders took their field trip to one of the missions, who got to tell the story? I imagine you can guess. We toured for two hours and visited nine key locations in the complex, of which only one was devoted to the indigenous community who stewarded the land before the arrival of the Spanish. We were told the names of Spaniard after Spaniard—Father Who-See-Foot and Father So-and-So. But not a single indigenous person was named. Not a single indigenous story was told. Thousands upon thousands of lives were simply collapsed into a 25-by-35-foot room displaying some features of their life together before missionization. All this was done with a tone of the benign. What did it matter if the way these children were being informed would actually leave them malformed?

On a car ride the day after the field trip I asked Riley a question. It's one we return to often as we try to help our kids understand something as layered and complex as injustice. The question is a ritual of ours, one your family can adopt as well. It moves with us as we talk about the California missions, or our school, or our neighborhood, or our church. We simply ask:

Whose story is being told, and whose is missing?

Kids experience storytelling all around them, in many forms. They can identify which of the characters in a plot gets to lead, gets to do the best jobs, or has the coolest powers. We can hone this skill for the sake of seeing the inequities in the world more clearly. The first few conversations you have with this question may take some nudging from you, but with practice, as the ritual repeats, your kids will become more equipped to answer on their own. Ultimately, it will become a question they carry within themselves, asking it not only about the history they're taught but the meetings they join or the faith communities they gather with.

SERVING WITHOUT SAVIORISM

Right after finishing seminary, my husband, Curtis, and I joined the youth ministry staff of a large church. As the middle school pastor, he would regularly take a group of students downtown to partner with a ministry that served various Los Angeles neighborhoods. The strategy was simple: Show up every Saturday with groceries and diapers. Enjoy conversation with the neighbors. Repeat. The key was consistency—the group never missed a Saturday.

Over time, we became more connected to the neighborhood's site leader, Beto. Short, tan, and highly tattooed, Beto's experience as a lifelong Angeleno, his years in a gang, and then no longer in a gang, along with his inspiring and empathetic personal skills, all meant he was perfectly placed to understand the complexities of the neighborhood, which also happened to be the largest public housing project in L.A., with nearly ten thousand residents.

And here we come, two bright-eyed youth pastors with a dozen suburban white kids from an *extremely* affluent community. (Like, an-off-ramp-away-from-the-Kardashians rich.) Ready to help! Ready to serve! Ready to save the neighborhood!

Our students had a saviorism mentality: the notion that their help, even their very presence, was what this community needed. Saviorism says that the neighborhood would not be okay without them, the saviors. It overlooks the assets right within the community and assumes that an outsider is better suited to solve problems than the people who call the place home. I don't blame our students for thinking this way. It is the paradigm that white cultured US churches have operated from for so long, from the missionary movement to suburban megachurches planting in urban contexts without contextualizing.

Nevertheless, the saviorism was prevalent and needed correcting. Could we help our students grow in understanding poverty, racism, and justice such that they could serve without saviorism?

Not only does saviorism risk hurting the very community we hope to help, it often ties us right back into contractual moralism. Part of what we do to ensure the protection of the god of moralism is to "help the less fortunate." There's an entire version of contractual moralism built less on the personal piety of honesty or responsibility and more on being ambassadors for causes, activists who vote just right. But justice-seeking is such long-term work, not the up-and-to-the-right work we tend to celebrate as a culture. Disillusionment and weariness will come for any of us who serve justice like a god instead of the God who is just.

Saviorism…

- Sounds like, "They have so little, but they're so joyful," or "It just makes me so grateful for what I have."
- Cares about the smiles in the moment without attending to solutions for the long term.
- Focuses on photo ops that will make great IG profile pics.
- Makes heroes out of the drop-in group: "We are just so proud of these kids for giving up their Saturday to help."

Serving without saviorism…

- Defers to the needs the local community identifies, whether they make good photo ops or not.
- Is careful about public storytelling, online and beyond, respecting the dignity of the community that calls this space home and knows it best.
- Leaves a short-term interaction saying, "We all deserve to have enough of what we need and some to share. How do I help that happen? How do I hurt that effort?"
- Frames the drop-in group appropriately, as learners and guests.

We knew we'd found a great partner in Beto when he told us, "I just really love serving with the suburban kids. I can't imagine—you have all this stuff, the sports and big house and fancy clothes. I didn't have any of that stuff. And to have all that stuff, and still be so sad, and there's so much mental health stuff happening, and all that. I just feel for them."

Their parents would have been insulted by this reflection. But he was spot-on. These students were paying "the price of privilege," as Madeline Levine describes, carrying high anxiety, feeling pressure to perform and extreme loneliness, and taking on riskier behaviors by the month. As Beto welcomed, loved, and included our students, he gifted them a space where they could grow in experiencing kinship and seeking justice rather than serving to alleviate shame or be the saviors.

Each of these practices shares a common commitment as it relates to injustice: the commitment to tell the truth. Injustice is perpetuated by manipulation, deceit, and spinning the story. Anchoring to a God who is just requires us to be relentlessly committed to telling the truth, however messy it is.

Our faith can handle any messy truth. Because naming the truth is the heart of confession. Confession is naming what really is. What was really said. What was really done. After confession there can be mending. Repairing. Reimagining. Restoring. Something new can be made after the truth is named. So we tell the truth. And we tell our kids the age-appropriate truth. And, as we do, our just God is with us.

CONSIDER

What are you already doing, individually or as a family, that helps you experience God's justice, especially the way it points to the person? How could that be leaned into, tweaked, or expanded?

What sort of experiment can you try first in order to make anchoring in and experiencing the justice of God part of your family's life?

CHAPTER 8

God Is Joyful

Once, back when I was in grad school, I was enjoying a break from studying. Naturally, this took the form of a day at the beach. It was relatively mild, if memory serves, one of those days when the sun isn't beating down angrily so much as shyly peeking out from behind its blanket of clouds. Down the beach to my right was a family with one child, a girl around four or five years old.

I didn't pay much attention to them until late in the day when something caught the corner of my eye. I looked over to see their daughter running around in circles, arms straight out, blond hair streaming back behind her. Whether she was pretending to be a plane, a bird, a superhero, or a pteranodon, I couldn't tell you, but what I can say with certainty is that she was loving every second of it, her face a picture of delight, her laughter sounding clearly over the crashing waves.

And she just kept going, minute after minute, circles becoming loops becoming figure eights. I watched her go and go, a smile creeping slowly onto my face, whatever stress I was feeling in the midst of studying and books and finals and essays powerless before the pure, unadulterated joy of what I was watching.

What I was seeing wasn't the result of achieving something, or producing something, or accomplishing something. The beauty and value of it all was pure, purposeless play, an overwhelming delight in the wonder of sand, water, breeze, and clouds that just couldn't be held in any longer.

In stark contrast was a day a few years ago, sitting in counseling in Illinois, a fluffy pillow on my lap, the sky solid gray out the large window. "I have a complicated relationship with happy," I confessed. Happy felt selfish and overindulgent. But the lack of play in my life was taking an obvious toll on my trust in God. I am inclined to work hard to get things just right, but I didn't want to anymore, and I wondered if perhaps God didn't want that either. Nevertheless, I worried that God tsk-tsked me when I did things just for the fun of it.

What is it about growing up that results in our losing the capacity for delight and wonder? Where does that unselfconscious ability to enjoy play without feeling guilty go? The child psychologists out there could surely give a more complete answer about the ways we're socialized out of joy. The church historian, too, could share insights about some of the Western sensibilities about holiness that squashed a lot of the fun out of life. As for me, I'm convinced that part of the answer goes back to a pervasive myth we've touched on already: that joy is beside the point, because of obedience.

Verses like Hebrews 12:11, "All discipline for the moment seems not to be joyful, but sorrowful; yet to those who have been trained by it, afterwards it yields the peaceful fruit of righteousness" (NASB), seem to say that fun is a distraction from discipleship, a selfish pursuit undermining a spiritual one. We're supposed to suffer, not have fun. Look no further than the heated debate as to whether it's appropriate for Christians...to dance. Gasp! (My Christian college allowed dancing, and I learned that to some undergraduates from holier schools this was a sure sign that we didn't take faith seriously.)

But the Bible, unlike some Christians, doesn't present a contrast between long-term formation and joy. In fact, joy is, throughout Scripture, an essential component of our formation. It is the fruit of God's Spirit working in us, alongside patience and peace and all the rest. Paul tells the Philippians to "rejoice in the Lord always; again I will say, rejoice!" (Phil. 4:4 NASB). When the prophets in the Old Testament drew a picture of the future day when God would act to save Israel and usher in the glorious kingdom of God, one of the most common words used to describe that day was "joyful." Why? Because our God is a joyful God.

And just as it takes practice to connect to God's peace and God's patience, so, too, it takes practice to connect with God's joy. We may think, *But how could the practice of joy possibly be an unpleasant discipline?* Well, have you ever experienced being stuck in a negative script and, if you're honest, wanting to stay there? There was a long stretch of several months when my kids were preschoolers and the script of the morning was "We are always running late and if *you all* would please just hurry, this wouldn't have to happen!" Joyful mornings felt unrealistic and, honestly, the blame script was more comfortable than the discipline of crafting a new, lighter morning routine. Sometimes complaining or anxiety are just easier places to wallow when compared to the work of making room for joy. Joy doesn't just happen; it takes practice. But the practice is worthwhile, as it helps us anchor to our joyful God.

Our problem is not that joy distracts us from something more spiritual, but rather that we have narrowed what counts as spiritual to obedience and sacrificed joy in the process. Why is that? Why is joy overlooked? What is it that causes us to shy away from joy as a critical aspect of our faith culture?

CONSIDER

Do you ever have a complicated relationship with happy? How might that impact your own view of God's character?

As a kid, I was around a lot of golf. I even attended a golf camp for a week one summer. So allow me to use an image from the golf course to help describe what's going on here. (Don't worry, non-golfers, I promise it'll make sense.) When someone begins a hole of golf, the first thing they do is to look out at the course ahead for danger, what golfers call hazards—places they don't want the ball to go. Two common hazards are sand traps and water. Even if you know next to zero about golf, you can imagine that it's unhelpful to a game whose purpose is to move the tiny golf ball from one spot to another to have that ball stuck in a pit of sand or under the water.

As we look out at the golf course of our faith, similarly, there are two hazards we might see between us and our goal, joy. First is the trap of idolizing happiness, such that *it*, not following Jesus, becomes the point of religion. This takes us back to the element of moralistic *therapeutic* deism; believing that the purpose of religiosity is personal comfort or ease. There is an underlying selfishness to this trap, whereas God's goal is joy for all. Paradoxically, pursuing only personal happiness often means we are not a joyful people. I can't pursue happiness that is just for me and not something we all enjoy.

If the first trap idolizes happiness, the second reacts against it. This is the trap of despondency, when we look at the injustice and suffering of the world and think that joy is inappropriate for those who care about such things. In light of the world's pain, how could a person celebrate? Fun is selfish and shows a lack of seriousness about the problems that need solving. Instead, we should commit ourselves to *do-goodery*, tirelessly devoting ourselves to tackling systemic change. Do-goodery—even when the good is important and the goals worthy—can still be a form of moralism, one that idolizes justice-seeking. Other moralistic systems may make a list of personal choices, like being honest or being responsible, but do-goodery is no less list-centric, with items telling us to recycle, and not to buy fast fashion or anything from Amazon, or at least feel very guilty if we do.

God's joy goes beyond moralistic justice-seeking that is an end unto itself. Left to itself, do-goodery, just like moralistic therapeutic list-maintenance, leaves us weary and discouraged. But God's joy renews the justice-loving, righteousness-seeking people of God so that the pursuit is life-giving and joy-filled, even as it's essential and serious work. After all, the world we're hoping for, the one God is restoring, will be distinctly joyful.

Anchoring to a God who is joyful offers us a path down the

fairway (the short-grassed middle of a golf hole without hazards—I got you, non-golf folks). God's joy goes beyond mere therapeutic religiosity, especially insofar as it marks a community. God's people, connected to God's joy, do wild things that are possible only when you trust in the joyful abundance of God. Generosity is risky, but joy is what gives us the security to take the risk. We can move beyond our own personal comfort-seeking and toward abundance-trusting generosity because God isn't simply caring for us, God is seeking joy for us.

And on the other side, God's joy is more than just the fuel for justice work but also a good in and of itself. It isn't a reward to be earned, like a pizza party for being the first-place team. Joy is a marker of the kingdom among us, a new reality that we're invited to access at all times, simply because it matches who God is.

So let's visit a wedding at Cana, where we reconnect to God's joy. For kids, I tell the story from John like this:

One time, in a town called Cana, there was a wedding. Two people were getting married, and they invited their whole community to come celebrate with them, including Jesus and his disciples. Just like at a party now, weddings then had special foods, music, laughing, and special drinks. You might like lemonade or soda for a special drink. They liked wine.

Since the wedding party was for a big group, a big problem came up (at least, it was a big problem when the goal was a great celebration): They ran out of wine. Why was that a big problem? Because the party would be over. All done. End of celebration.

Jesus' mom, Mary, was at the wedding, and she went to Jesus and said, "They ran out of wine!"

At first, Jesus' answer sounds even a little bit sassy: "What does that have to do with me?" Jesus was saying that it wasn't really his concern.

And yet, Mary went to the workers and told them, "Whatever my son, Jesus, says for you to do, listen to him."

Despite what Jesus said to his mom, he went to the workers and said, "Fill these six jars with water." The jars were huge! Often a jug of milk in the refrigerator is one gallon. Well, in this case, each jar was big enough for twenty or thirty of those milk jugs! Filled up, they weighed more than you do!

When the jugs had been filled with water, Jesus told a worker to scoop some out and take it to the person in charge of the party, and have them drink.

Can you imagine how the worker might have felt? Perhaps he felt worried. After all, as far as the worker knew, he was bringing a ladleful of plain water to the person in charge of this huge wedding party! Maybe he thought he'd be in trouble: Why would the person in charge want a drink of plain water? Maybe he felt curious about what Jesus was doing.

When the person in charge tasted what was brought to him, he tasted not water, but wine! Good, delicious wine! And he said, "You know, usually people serve the good things first and the less-good things later when people don't care so much. You saved the best for last!"

What had happened? Between the jug and the taste test, Jesus had turned the water into wine! So, so much wine—150 milk jugs full of wine. Instead of the party having to end, it could go on and on.

Anytime Jesus does a miracle, we should ask: Why? What does this miracle help us see about who God is or what God is doing in the world? If Jesus turned water into wine at this wedding, what does that tell us about what God is like?

It shows us that God is a joyful God, and the community of God should be joyful, a place of more-than-enoughness.

John tells us this story, putting it right at the top of his narrative to answer this question: What can we expect of this kingdom of God that Jesus is announcing?

If we carry on with a moral-of-the-story approach, we don't hear John's account with the ears we're meant to listen with. Instead of wondering: *What life are we invited to live with and because of Jesus?* we would instead say: *What did the people at the wedding get right or wrong about obedience?* The latter question will leave us talking about the obedience of the servants who were sent for the water. They listened to Jesus and did what he said, and so should you.

Back to John's real questions: What's this new reality he claims to be ushering in like? It's like a huge party with an abundance of wine. I don't want us to miss the heart of this story: Jesus does this miracle for the purpose of keeping the party going.

The point of the miracle is joy. The point of including the story in the gospel narrative is joy. Flat-out—throw your head back to clear the way for the belly laugh—joy. The wedding is not a break before the people get back to the real work of being a holy people; to live with joy *is* to be holy. Holiness, remember, is about being distinct, set apart, different. It was true then and it's true now: To live with real joy is a holy way to live.

Joy is an end in itself, a good in itself, because it is a marker of God's presence. We often look for God's presence to do something, change something, fix something. Sometimes that's the case. However, sometimes God's presence is simply meant to be enjoyed. Perhaps our hesitancy about joy reveals that we don't think God actually delights in us, so we can't imagine a God who is fine with our just plain having a good time. But that seems to be the case in this story. Jesus is there to help his community have a good time.

SPIRAL THE ATTRIBUTE

In addition to the story of the wedding at Cana, here are some ideas for spiraling back to God's joy in other parts of the Bible:

- Festivals: As God's people are being reformed, after the exodus, through the law, God tells them to host multiple festivals during the year. These feasts would be community-wide parties that included everyone and anchored the people to God's joy, abundance, and grace toward them as they retold stories of who God had been for them.
- Jesus' lost-and-found parables point to God's particular joy when people come back home to God. Bringing them home again is not a project God resents, groveling at the lost state of humanity. It's a purpose God devotes Themself to and delights in its realization.

> - If learning Bible verses is part of your family's web, consider including verses like Nehemiah 8:10: "The joy of [Yahweh] is your strength" (NASB); or Zephaniah 3:17: "For the LORD your God is living among you. [God] is a mighty savior. [God] will take delight in you with gladness. With [Their] love, [God] will calm all your fears. [God] will rejoice over you with joyful songs" (NLT).

I once asked a large group of parents what they hoped to pass on to their kids when it came to faith. The overwhelming response orbited around this theme: unconditionality. They hoped their kids really knew what grace was, that truly nothing could make them more or less loved. What makes joy so powerful is its ability to help a person feel grace in their bones. "Joy is what we feel when we're grateful for the grace given to us," writes Pastor Ben Patterson. I wonder if it also works in the opposite direction?

Grace is what we know is true when we've been able to live with joy.

What Patterson describes isn't linear: Grace to gratitude to joy. He rightly names the link among all three. Practicing gratitude will cause us to understand grace and live with more joy. Starting with joy will spark gratitude and deepen grace. They are all interconnected; they're woven together.

Perhaps no attribute of God's has been more tossed aside by the myth of obedience training as God being joyful. The assumption that the purpose of Christian parenting is to raise "good kids" costs us, and our kids, a deep connection to God's joy, because if the point is to be good, even when we don't want to, where does that leave fun? What good is fun?

Fun is a pathway to grace. What a wonderful God to be inviting us all into joyful, abundant life.

KID DATES

Set aside a consistent block of time and begin a tradition of Kid Dates. The activities you do will depend on your kid and context. You might visit their favorite park, catch a movie out or have a movie night in (popcorn in both cases, please!), or there might be a place they'd love to eat or a game they'd love to play.

My husband and I also use Kid Dates as a chance to spend individual time with each child. We often bring a portable game, like cards, to a dessert spot of their choosing. For a while our local mini golf spot had a great deal on a pass, so you'd always find us there on a Friday night. Another family I know keeps it simple with the same options: Go for a walk, go to a park, pick a board game. The dates are for ninety minutes every other week, and the child always knows they can pick from one of those three activities.

SAY THE BEAUTIFUL TRUTH

As representatives of the joy of God in our families, we recognize that there is simply no such thing as delighting too much in our children on God's behalf. As Macrina Wiederkehr says, "Oh God, help us to believe the truth about ourselves, no matter how beautiful it is." When it comes to how we as adults approach our kids, this also means, "God, help us to believe the truth about this child, no matter how beautiful it is."

Recently Riley has taken to telling me, "I knooow. You say that all the tiiiime."

What do I say?

"I love you so much." "I'm so glad God gave you to me and that I get to be your mom." "You are such a terrific kid."

I know. How dare I?

I am all in on telling my kids how much they delight me and how they are a gift from God to our family. If they are rolling their eyes and drawing out their vowels as they say they already knoooow that, I might almost have said it enough.

Often joy bubbles up in the hearts of our children simply because we *say the words*. Out loud. Often.

What words does your child hear from you that tell them they are a source of delight? Maybe you already have some commonly said phrases, or maybe you can take a minute right now and think of how you would say that to your child.

START A JOY COLLECTION

On my entry table are two mason jars full of shells, collected small handfuls at a time from Southern California beaches: Corona del Mar, the Long Beach pier, Bolsa Chica. On my best friend's mantel there's a jar of sea glass from Lake Michigan, in the colors of green, brown, and the rarely found and therefore most celebrated, blue.

Shells and sea glass aren't merely collections. They are mementos of delight, carted home after a day spent out in the world God made, with the people God gave us to raise, playing. They are joy collections, reminding us all of the overwhelming goodness God has infused into the world. Our hearts lift when we notice joy because we were made for it. What's more, so was everybody else. The shells don't invite me to escape my life for the beach, they remind me what is in my real life, and what I hope, in some small, real way, to help create for others: deep joy.

Maybe you need to start a joy collection, for yourself or with your kid. What you collect is entirely up to you and need not make sense to another person, so long as it reminds you: You trust a God who is joyful.

INCREASE THE FUZZ FACTOR

It surprises me every time, though by now it shouldn't, how many adults expect faith to grow well using methods that aren't fun. But fun is the language of a child, and as Fred Rogers reminded us, "Play is the work." More specifically, play is a powerful tool to cultivate family warmth.

YOUR KID ASKS

Does God toot?

Far from irreverent, wondering about God in silly ways models God's joy. So you might say, "Of course! Jesus was a person, God in a body, a human just like us. All humans toot, so Jesus tooted! What I wonder is if Jesus ever practiced crossing his eyes just for the fun of it."

This kind of imagination that invites kids to practice trusting God really is joyful, and spiritual things are not exclusively serious.

As I mentioned in chapter 2, family warmth, the simple joy of being together, the felt experience of closeness, connection, understanding, and care, is an aspect of faith development all its own. The study that drew this out—a massive long-term study of families—found that a pivotal dynamic for nurturing faith is family bonds. It's unsurprising that relational connections play a key role in a kid's faith experience, but what we may not realize is just how important relationships are, and that the quality of the relationships is key. Family warmth is as simple as whatever cultivates fuzzies in your family. It's the fuzz factor.

If we limit what "counts" as a faith practice to things that seem overtly Christian—prayer, Bible reading, church attendance, and the like—we miss the chance to nurture faith through the fuzz factor. When our family plays tickle monster or board games, has a dance party, draws side by side, or has our favorite dinner just because, we are embodying what we believe to be true about the God we trust. We are living the way people would live if they really believed God was joyful.

GENEROSITY AND MORE-THAN-ENOUGH-NESS; OR...LET'S TALK TITHE

Before anyone shuts this book in a panic ("I *knew* there was a catch with this whole joy thing!"), let's look briefly at a verse from

Deuteronomy. Deuteronomy 14:26 says this when explaining what the people should do with the commanded tithe: "You may spend the money for whatever your heart desires: for oxen, or sheep, or wine, or strong drink, or *whatever your heart desires*; and there you shall eat in the presence of [Yahweh] your God and rejoice, you and your household" (NASB, emphasis added).

God gives us more than enough, not to sustain us, not so we might anxiously muddle through, but so that we might rejoice, so that we might be filled with life and freedom and joy. This verse quite literally tells us to take some of our tithe money and buy ourselves a rib eye and a nice bottle of whiskey—at least that's how my husband would use it. However, it gives us this freedom with one caveat, that we would rejoice *before Yahweh* as we eat and drink it. This isn't hedonism; it's a spiritual practice.

The image in Deuteronomy is of Yahweh as a king who demands a small percentage—10 percent was far less than what the gods and kings of the other nations required—and then turns right around and *gives it back* so that we might enjoy the gifts of God *with* God. Our God of joy sets up the tithe, in part, so that we would connect to joy ourselves.

All this is hard to translate from a once-a-year harvest feast to our own context, but it seems safe to say that we are invited into a practice of setting aside a portion of what God has given us, at some regular interval, to buy whatever we want and then consciously enjoy it in the presence of God. Far from being a party for its own sake, it's a practice that helps us remember how our stuff can shape our joy.

I'd be remiss to stop here, though. We must notice that the tithe is also used to help others join in. Scholars point out that it would be virtually impossible to consume 10 percent of the harvest in one meal, no matter how lavish. The rest of the tithe is to be dedicated to the Levite, the foreigner, the orphan, and the widow. The ones who have no harvest, no source of income, the ones who don't have enough—they are to be fully included in the abundance and the joy, for they are the ones God holds in high regard and watches over.

The foreigner, orphan, and widow are people who have no harvest because they have either lost their land due to misfortune, mismanagement, or the death of their patriarch, or perhaps they have left their homeland as refugees. They have no way of participating in the broader economy and supporting themselves. But God's vision is for a community whose more than enough becomes all having more than enough. That's who our God is, and so that's who God's people should be.

This transforms our generosity from an act of charity—in the sense of giving something out of our benevolence to those less fortunate than ourselves—to an enactment of what is true of the kingdom of God, namely, that all have the right to experience the joy and abundance of God. It is the responsibility of the people of God who have more than enough to remember to help the whole community join in the enjoyment of God's abundance.

The tithe can be a practice that helps us avoid both traps, and inviting our kids into it early on forms their views on money, generosity, abundance, and community. Each gift can, on the one hand, draw us away from idolizing personal happiness and reconnect us with others; and on the other hand, give us hope for the change that gift makes possible (this is especially true with collective giving, like with a faith community or even just a few other families).

As we develop family practices to nurture joy, we demonstrate our belief that God is joyful. As we live generously, it's because it spreads joy to others.

The way forward from my complicated relationship with happy was not to force myself to see spiritual activities as fun, but to help myself see that fun activities are spiritual. I wasn't giving God credit for the warmth of a belly laugh, the way a memory of a funny story could bring a smile well after it was told, or how our own chests swell whenever we are part of joy's expansion to another person. I was looking askance at fun and needed new eyes, for when a Christian person looks askance at fun, it means we've failed to recognize that Jesus chose to make wine. He chose it. Not to teach a lesson about being obeyed, but to demonstrate a deep truth about his mission. It was a joy for Jesus to provide an abundance of wine, because that is what God's like. Let's take care not to snub the wedding feast in the name of being saintly.

GO BIG FOR BIRTHDAYS

How do you celebrate birthdays in your family? Does the special person pick their meal or how a day will be spent? Who else joins in to celebrate with you? The joy of a birthday makes it a perfect opportunity to lean in to God's joy, creating traditions and fostering relationships. However you mark the day, consider that God's joy might nudge you to go big. Big doesn't have to mean expensive; it just means giving care and attention to the celebrated person. Celebrate the adults, as well as the kids. Including adults in this also helps kids practice creating joy for others' sakes.

CONSIDER

What are you already doing, individually or as a family, that helps you experience God's joy? How could that be leaned into, tweaked, or expanded?

What sort of experiment can you try first in order to make anchoring in and experiencing the joy of God part of your family's life?

CHAPTER 9

God Is With Us

"There really isn't any proof for God," my then eight-year-old son said from the back seat. Car time is our best time for faith conversations, and we've been intentional about encouraging those in ways big and small. But in the moment, rather than welcoming his honest thought, I felt my heart rate speed up involuntarily—was he announcing a conclusion of some sort? I managed a curious tone despite my nerves: "Say more about what you mean, kiddo."

"Well, like, you can't see God, or touch him, or hear him. *You* say God's real and close to us, but I can't really *know* that. There's no proof."

My science-minded, dinosaur-loving boy would love some

five-senses-based proof. But the type of proof he desperately wanted simply isn't available. Instead, I have stories, full of mystery but from trustworthy people who experienced what seems impossible without the presence of God. I told him one of those, of a family member's journey from addiction to sobriety. It's an untidy, holy story (as all healing stories are) that began when God gave a message to a pastor who knew nothing of that family member.

Then I told him what I believe: that the closest we have to proof are the stories of God's presence. That often people experience God's presence subtly, and yet they have a sense of God's nearness, God's leading, or God's comfort.

I can't help but notice how seldom stories like the one I told Riley are talked about in Christian circles. Perhaps in the interest of providing rock-solid proof, we've elevated stories of the sensational, where God's presence is described with terms like "undeniable" or "evident." And that's fine, so far as it goes, but the downside comes when we overlook stories of the ordinary, where God's presence might be described instead as "quiet nearness" or "courage for the day." The result is that many of us don't know what the still, small voice of God sounds like, and whether it even "counts," let alone how to help our kids hear it. We aren't sure how to live connected to God's presence ourselves, even though we want to, and, even more, we want to invite our kids into a day-to-day experience of God too.

What's more, if the only stories deemed worthy of being told are the amazing and stupendous, that communicates something to anyone whose experience of God has fallen a bit short of mind-blowing: Either "Something must be wrong with me" or "God isn't actually with me." Neither is true, but it's not hard to see how someone would draw such conclusions if their own story of noticing God's nearness feels less dramatic than the ones we amplify.

As we talked about earlier, there's a word for the belief that God is more far away than close at hand: deism. The deistic idea of a far-off god didn't appear in our understanding out of nowhere. The door was cracked open for it, at least in part, by a common (mis)understanding of sin—that one of sin's consequences is separation between God and humanity. You may have seen one of those sketches of two stick figures—humanity and God—standing on imposing cliffs with an uncrossable chasm in between, until the cross gets drawn in like a bridge. Or, as one kid's Christmas resource I saw once read: "Sin meant God had gone away; Christmas means God is here to stay." This idea that sin means God has left us largely alone and now observes us from a distance is, to put it bluntly, simply not one the Old Testament supports.

Right after the story of sin entering the world, after all, God comes near to Adam and Eve and clothes them. At the end of the story, they are far from the garden, but not God. The very next chapter features God coming near to Cain for a challenging conversation. Cain's sin doesn't make God go away; rather, it brings God close, in the hope of leading Cain to honesty about his wrong. Ultimately, Cain is the one who initiates leaving God's presence.

Although, really, the Old Testament calls into question whether leaving God's presence is even possible at all. Psalm 139 declares that there's nowhere one could go that is not in God's presence. The ark of the covenant is a tangible symbol of God's being among the people. Jonah tried desperately, futilely, to escape the presence of Yahweh God.

Yes, sin impacts humanity's relationship to God, both as individuals and as a collective. But even before Jesus comes, even despite sin's best efforts, God is not far away and separate. It simply is not true that "a holy God cannot be in the presence of sin." A holy God cannot be overcome by the power of sin, and so can come as near to the people God loves as They would like. Which is to say, right among us.

How, then, might we help our kids anchor to a God who is not far, but with us? How can we help them navigate the reality that there isn't proof, and yet there's presence? Let's turn to one story where God's presence is visible, if not exactly tangible.

God's people found themselves facing the desert, the edge of Egypt behind them, newly freed from slavery. God had come to rescue them, and now it was time to go. Even though there was a shorter route out of there, it was through a risky area, and God thought the people might hightail it back to Egypt if things got too hard too soon. (God was right about this. As the story goes on, we see that when life was difficult or scary, it was also difficult to get rid of that nagging suspicion that maybe slavery wasn't so bad after all.) So God led the people toward the Red Sea.

"By day," the Bible tells us, "[Yahweh] went ahead of them in a pillar of cloud to guide them on their way and by night in a pillar of fire to give them light, so that they could travel by day or night. Neither the pillar of cloud by day nor the pillar of fire by night left its place in front of the people" (Exod. 13:21–22 NIV).

At least, not until they needed it to.

Pharaoh had agreed to let the people go only after Yahweh had put God's own power on display. But once the dust settled, Pharaoh changed his mind, again. He gathered his chariots and soldiers and chased the Israelites down, which is how they found themselves with a sea on one side and an army on the other, unsure what to do. Remember that part about wanting to return to Egypt? That's just what they said, that they may as well have stayed enslaved instead of dying in the desert.

But God was with them. The pillar of cloud moved behind the Israelites, blocking the armies of Pharaoh from them. They were protected by God's presence until they could escape through the sea, because God split the waters for them to walk through.

God not only came to free them, but God came to be with them. As they left the Red Sea for the desert, they would look back not only on God's power but also on God's presence. God was with them. And God would be with them.

The people enter the desert, newly freed, but in a situation just as precarious. Every step takes them farther from the food supply of Egypt, farther from the flow of the Nile, farther from security, even if that security was inextricably tied to suffering. It's no surprise that they struggle to believe that they will be okay as they walk into the unknown.

PRESENT IN ALL PLACES

Our ability to empathize with the Israelites' uncertainty grows when we remember that the common understanding in the ancient Near East was that a deity's dominion was limited to a territory. Egypt's gods were powerful in Egypt, over its rain and its fertility. The desert ahead was something of a no-man's-land, so it made sense to wonder if it was also a no-god's-land, a place where they would be left on their own to fend for themselves.

Yet Yahweh God of Israel is not bound to one territory or limited by borders. The radical belief of the Old Testament is that God has dominion in all places—Egypt, the desert, the Promised Land, and even the lands to which Israel would later be exiled. God is always there, and, what's more, God chooses to come near. Cloud by day. Fire by night.

God's Presence Protects Them

When Pharaoh changes his mind and sends his army to chase down the Israelites, the pillar of cloud moves behind Israel, protecting them from their enemies. God's protection isn't offered in the abstract, through a change in their circumstance that could equally be called coincidence: "And just then, Pharaoh remembered he had left the fire burning in the royal bedroom, and his armies headed on home." In this story, God's protection is offered through God's presence. Egypt is blocked from Israel because God Themself moves between them, not unlike what God does for humanity in Christ when the forces of evil come to claim us.

God's Presence Leads Them

The cloud and the fire literally led the people out of Egypt, guiding them in the direction they should go. This often becomes a metaphor for us, that we, too, should follow God with our decisions along life's path. But the people literally spent the day following God, who wanted to lead them to a literal land where they could settle down, become rooted, and enjoy the fruit of that rootedness. (I can't help but notice how the descriptions of the Promised Land echo those of the garden. God dreams of our everyday lives lived in lovely places, each moment marked by a sense of God's nearness.) Fast-forward to Jesus' arrival, and the invitation he gives is literally "Follow me."

Pausing to remember this was an actual journey can be especially helpful when we look ahead a bit to the Old Testament law. If we jump too readily to a metaphorical leading, where the *real* point is to make good decisions, we may also view the law as a list of rules to follow in order to make those good decisions. This is not a good summary of the law. Contrary to how the law is represented at times, Israel is not led by a list of rules, but by God's own presence. In literally following God to that place, they are meant to grow their trust in Yahweh God alone. They come to love God through what God did to free them, bringing them out of slavery, bringing them through the sea, bringing them to the land. The literal leading is the backdrop for how the law does work, as a grateful response to the grace and faithfulness of Yahweh.

God's Presence Reshapes Them

For generations the Hebrews were a people controlled. In Egypt, Pharaoh dictated every detail of their lives, orienting their efforts toward his own glory and comfort. On the surface, it would be easy to think God does the same in the Old Testament, giving a law that looks to dictate every detail so the people will glorify God. But this is a misunderstanding of both the substance and purpose of the law, which is instead meant to provide a commentary for how this group of ancient Israelites might love God and one another in their particular time and place. God is with them to help them release a control-based existence and replace it with a trust-based one.

CONSIDER

Which of the aspects of God's presence that the story of the exodus highlights resonates most with you?

The law answers, for their context: Since God is with us, really with us, how do we all live together in ways that reflect that reality? Now, in our very different time and place, the specifics of that answer can feel confusing, even wrong. The distance, both in time and in culture, between the ancient Near East and the twenty-first-century West is vast. So we do well to time-hop, so to speak, entering into the story (and make no mistake, the law is part of the story) on its own terms.

SPIRAL THE STORY

In addition to focusing on God's power, here are some ideas for spiraling back to the story of the pillars of cloud and fire with a God-centered storytelling approach:

- God cares for us. As God leads and protects the people, they are experiencing a God who cares about them and shows up to demonstrate it.
- God frees us. This story is part of the larger story of the exodus, which will shape Israel's understanding of themselves: We are the freed ones. So much of how God's people are meant to live together comes

---

> from this identity. Later on, it will help shed light on what Jesus' resurrection means for the world too.
>
> - God is patient. The people are far from grateful through this experience, and yet God carries on, protecting them, guiding them, and sticking with them.

And so we're back to presence, which serves to reshape these people who have been controlled into people who choose to love God and one another. Yahweh God is reshaping the people from being controlled to choosing to trust. Despite being worthy of whatever form of allegiance God might desire, able to demand whatever obedience God wishes, God chooses to go first, being ever present with the people so they can grow in trust.

If all this is available because God is with us, how do we access it? It can seem unrealistic, at a minimum, when our days start with "Are you dressed? Peanut butter or turkey for your lunchbox? Yogurt or toast for breakfast? Time for your morning checklist!" If I need stretches of calm and quiet to connect with God's presence, well, let's just say that can be a long time coming.

But even as life moves along, we can not only be mindful that God is near, but also experience God's leading and reshaping of our own lives and the culture of our family. It happens when we practice noticing God's nearness.

I was recently introduced to Merlin Bird ID, the app I didn't know I needed, but absolutely do. Created by Cornell University, the app identifies the various birds chirping around you, which is how I now know that a house finch is singing outside from my loquat tree. When many birds are singing at once, it can highlight them in pale yellow from the list of all the birds it has picked up on.

What fascinates me about the app, in particular, is its ability to hear a bird in my yard, which also has constant white noise from the freeway, the intermittent revving of engines (it's recently popular in my area to remove mufflers, so that's fun), and the regular passing by of planes from our nearby airport. Engine after engine roars around my house, and yet I tap "sound ID" and the app tunes in to just the songs of the birds, hiding in plain sight in the branches nearby.

Anchoring to a God who is with us is about finding the spiritual equivalent of Merlin Bird ID. It's about the practices, habits, or rhythms that help us notice the music of God's nearness amid the din of daily life. Like the birds in my yard, God is always there, and yet without tuning myself in to God's presence, I'm liable to go long stretches not hearing the song of love that's calling to me.

How might we go about helping our kids to do the same? What types of practices or family rhythms could anchor them to a God we can trust to be with us?

SET PRAYERS AND PATHWAYS

Our first home was situated in the midst of some low hills covered in brush and wild mustard, and if you walked straight to the back of the complex, you'd find a rocky, steep path inviting you to climb them. The path itself was a bit crooked, with ruts in the middle where the rain ran on the rare days it rained. Clearly it wasn't created by the parks department, but rather improvised by neighbors over time. Anytime you wanted some air, some quiet, and that sense of space Southern California rarely offers, the path was there. An invitation.

Predetermined prayers work much like that trail, I find. They don't need to be fancy or crafted, but having them there at the ready can help us find our way to God's presence. This is especially true in times of hardship.

We don't always remember that kids experience times of hardship (unless they, sadly, have gone through a particular trauma in life). But, as with adults, children have challenging seasons when they don't know how to pray. During periods of sadness or confusion, we can introduce a ritual of praying one set prayer that can serve as a path to God's presence.

Set prayers can be simple and short; they can address the situation at hand or speak more generally. You might create the prayer for your child, or they might want to create it themselves. You could take a verse from Scripture or a shared prayer from the Christian tradition. Like our trail, it doesn't need to be crafted and perfect. Find the words that fit, and then stick with them instead of searching for new ones.

For example:

- If school is difficult, you could pray a set prayer right before they go in that says, "God, as kiddo is in school today, help them know You are near and You care."
- If a sibling relationship is rocky, your child could pray a set prayer for the relationship like, "God, I don't always get along with [sibling]. You are patient and slow to get mad. Help me practice that, too, and when I'm not, thanks for helping us mend things and try again."

- If your child has a stumper of a faith question that won't be answered easily, you could have a set prayer about that very thing. In fact, this is what we did after that car conversation about proof. At bedtime, we had a set prayer of "God, Riley is having a hard time trusting that You're here when You can't be seen, touched, or heard like he hears me now. Would You help him know that's okay, and would You help him get to know You as he grows?"

A PRAYER YOU WEAR

When I worked at a megachurch, we were always looking for opportunities for kids to respond to God in more personal ways. Often, this meant providing them something they could wear after adding a customized detail. The materials were often simple and affordable (little-known fact: When you have to provide materials for hundreds of kids, the budget per kid is pretty small. Despite being a megachurch, my curriculum team had less than fifteen cents per kid per weekend to work with), but what mattered was the chance to make it personal.

Start with a neon paper wristband, then add some felt-tip pens and a question like:

- Who do you need God to be for you right now?
- What is one truth about God you want to remember this week?
- What was God like in this Bible story? Let's write down one or more of those traits to remind us God will be that for us too.

- Who can we be praying for? Let's write down their initials.
- Who does God say you are? Pick one or more words to answer that to remember this week.

Using a tangible, tailored reminder can invite kids to be in regular conversation with God in the days that follow. This is especially true when we remind them that these prayers can be short and don't need fancy language. One sentence as they line up from recess, a quick thought as they look in the mirror in the morning—these examples don't just make prayer more accessible to a kid, they point to the idea of spending the day aware of God's presence. And, speaking of God's presence…

EXAMEN

Perhaps you are already familiar with the Prayer of Examen, attributed to the Ignatian tradition of spiritual practices. It is a prayer focused around remembering in order to help us notice God's presence in our ordinary moments. We may not always notice God with us at the time, but by intentionally slowing down to look back, we can be better aware of, connect with, and respond to God's nearness.

There are a few templates for a traditional examen, and many "right" ways to engage this kind of prayer. Examen often flows in this way, more or less:

1. Begin by acknowledging God's presence with you, both in the moment you're in and in the moments you will

look back to remember. Take time to thank God for God's nearness and love.

2. Pray to ask God for insight as you prepare to remember back.

3. Review the day (you can of course do the week, or a season as well), noticing not only what happened, but the emotions attached to those events.

4. Respond to the events you remember. When did God seem near or far? Is there anything you remember you'd like to talk with God about?

5. Look forward and ask if there's anything God is leading you toward. Often this is less about a specific action to take and more about a posture with which you'll engage the next day.

Examen is an excellent tool to help kids notice God's presence, provided it's presented to them in accessible ways. To that end, here's my suggestion for maintaining the goal of examen (noticing and responding to God's presence) while adjusting the wording for a kid. Kids often need a couple of prompts to serve as a jumping-off point, so this guide is more verbose than the overview I just gave above. However, your own child may not need every question here to be able to reflect back prayerfully. You'll notice I've imagined this as a bedtime practice reviewing the day. It could also be great in the car after evening sports practice, or anytime your child is open to five minutes of introspection.

Say: I'm going to ask you some questions, and they are just for you to think about inside your mind. You don't have to tell me your answers, but you can if you want to.

There isn't a right or wrong way to answer any of these questions. Sometimes you may think or feel a lot, and sometimes you might not think or feel much at all. This is one way for us to practice noticing and listening to God.

1. First, let's take a big breath, imagining the air coming in is God's love. It's that close, filling us up.

   Just like the air is always here, God is always here. Just like we sometimes don't even notice how we've been breathing, we sometimes don't even notice God's with us. But when we stop and take a big breath, we notice again. We are going to spend a few minutes noticing God.

   Pray: "God, thank You that we are always with You and always loved."

2. Now, let's ask God to help us as we remember the day.

   Pray: "God, as we look back over today, would You help us notice You or anything important You want us to see? Amen."

3. What happened today? You might remember big stuff or small stuff. It's okay if you don't really remember all that happened now that the day is ending.

   Start in the morning as you woke up and started the day. What happened this morning?

   What about during the middle of the day? What happened then?

   Think about evening time, before we got to bedtime. What did you do this evening?

4. As you remember today, how did you feel? It's okay if you don't really know; just try to notice.

Were there any times you felt happy, light, or good inside?

Were there any times you felt sad, scared, nervous, lonely, or any other big feelings?

When was one time you felt especially close to God or loved by God?

When was one time you felt especially far from God or alone today?

5. Let's take ten seconds to be quiet with God to see if there's anything important for us to know or feel. It's okay if it just seems quiet and nothing special comes up.

Pray: "God, before we wrap up, if there is anything else You hope we think of or feel, we are practicing noticing." Then be quiet.

Close by praying: "Thank You, God, for this time with You. Help us remember how loved we are. Amen."

I wish there were a scientific-method-style proof involving all five-senses. What if the "proof" I do have—stories from our faith communities and Scripture; experiences of God's gentle, yet invisible presence; the testimony of creation—isn't enough for my child?

I want proof because I want to control the outcome. If I have proof, this sort of thinking tells me, certainly trust must follow. My fear is more precisely named as the inability to control whether or not my son will trust God. Ever since my kids were infants my prayer for them has been "God, may they trust You with their whole hearts for their whole lives." Whether circumstances are good or bad, stable or precarious, joyful or sorrowful, I hope they choose to trust God in the midst, and experience God with them in the midst. It's not that I worry that life's difficulties will make them "fall away";

it's that I believe God with us in those difficulties makes a world of difference in how we walk through them. I don't want my kids to miss out on the chance to face all of life's various seasons and situations with an awareness that they are not alone.

Of course, when I take these very fears to God myself, I am met with a similar response: I am not alone. No matter what happens, God will be with me.

CONSIDER

Have these or other practices been impactful for you in experiencing God's presence?

What are you doing that keeps you from experiencing God's presence? How can that be minimized, or ended altogether?

Which of the suggested ideas might you want to add to your family's life together? How might you need to adapt it so that it fits your real life?

What sort of experiment are you going to try first in order to make anchoring in and experiencing the presence of God part of your family life?

CHAPTER 10

Jesus Is Lord

To believe or not to believe...is not the question.

We've been looking at some of the key attributes of our God, trying to drill down on what the God we are inviting our kids to anchor to is like. We've spent so much time on this because one of the most important questions for us to ask, one that should be asked far more often in the church, is "Which god are you talking about, exactly?"

"Which god...?" may seem like a strange question, since our culture is one where monotheism has been the dominant theological perspective for so long. We're almost two millennia deep into the main question about God being framed as "Do you believe in

God?" with the assumed answer being a simple yes, no, or I don't know. But this is actually one way our current Western culture understands far less of the world than did the people of two thousand years ago. In the ancient world, no one would have framed the question as "Do you believe in God or not?" Instead, the question was "Which gods do you worship, and what are they like?"

In the Old Testament, the message is not that people *should* believe in God instead of *not* believing in God. The message is that people should believe in Yahweh, who is *different from* the other gods. These differences are the essence of what *holy* means— distinct, set apart, not like the others. Yahweh is a holy God *because* Yahweh offers life instead of death, a way of living that is characterized by joy and abundance and justice, which is very much not what the other gods were offering. That's the choice Moses, Joshua, the judges, and the prophets are encouraging the people to make: "Will you choose to trust Yahweh instead of some combination of Ra, Molech, Baal, Asherah, and others? Will you choose this one God, who is King of all the earth, and who is good?"

We may be tempted to think things are different today, that it is antiquated to talk about idolatry in our sophisticated, scientific culture. Idols seem superstitious, beneath our consideration, an interesting quirk of ancient religions. Nothing could be further from the truth. Despite our framing of the question as "believe in God or don't," when we look at how we actually live, we find that not much has changed in the past two thousand years. There are still a multitude of gods to choose from. And every human being is deciding, intentionally or not, which one(s) to trust. Idolatry is just as prevalent now as it was in the days of Moses.

Simply put, an idol is more than a figurine carved out of wood or cast out of metal; it is whomever or whatever I trust to protect and provide for me. In the ancient world, those were named beings—a water god and a sun god would provide what was needed for crops to grow. People would trust them to make sure they wouldn't starve. War gods would protect from enemies. Fertility goddesses would make sure the babies kept coming.

Having called Southern California home for nearly all my life, I've become deeply familiar with the reality of drought. In fact, we opted to replace our lawn with native, drought-tolerant flowers and succulents just a few months ago, thereby avoiding the fate of many of our neighbors: straw and dust yards, parched from the combination of 100-degree days and necessary limits on watering. I can imagine a world where drought meant far more than an ugly landscape, where it created tremendous fear within a person who could do nothing but trust...someone...to send the rain before it was too late. Whatever or whoever that someone was became their god, their idol.

In our modern world, the things we trust to protect and provide for us have different names or take different forms, but they are no less real. We have gods called "good education," "retirement plan," "personal network," and "health." Any of these, and more, can be an idol when they complete this sentence:

Whatever happens, it will all be okay because...

We all have our own reasons that it'll all be okay:

- because of how much I have in the bank, my home equity, my retirement accounts. I can rely on that. I've made responsible decisions, and as long as I keep doing that, everything will be fine.
- because the right people are in charge of our country, making the right decisions, appointing the right officials.

- because I'm a good person, and so surely good things will come my way too.
- because at least I have my family, and they will continue to give me meaning and purpose as I go through my days, even if other things don't go the way I want.
- because I am a hard worker, I'm self-sufficient, and I can take care of myself and those around me no matter what.
- because I plan ahead and won't be caught off guard.

What is particularly challenging about completing this sentence is the answers that come to us are almost certainly good things. They are likely important things. Worthy things to care about. Which leads us to questions that require deeper discernment: Are they good things that I could let go of? Or are they good things I've allowed to become my security in place of God? We are the only ones who can answer that for ourselves. But whatever our honest answer is, that's a clue as to what we worship.

As I was thinking about how I would, honestly, finish that sentence, the truth is that more than a little bit of me believes it'll be okay because I can fall back on some combination of hard work, privilege, and talent. I put way more trust than I should in those things. In other words, I have a foundational belief that whatever happens, whether things work out or not, I will be able to figure it out, make a way forward, because I can tap into those resources, so surely I will land on my feet on the other side.

But the testimony of the Bible, from back to front, from Genesis through the Prophets through the Gospels to Revelation, is that if your answer to that question is anything other than God, you're going to be disappointed. Bitterly. The idols always sound good, but they're also always empty. They might seem to work for a time, usually when things are going smoothly, but they can't save you, and they can't bring life to you, not reliably, not ultimately. They aren't worth your trust.

When the drought comes, you'll find that your roots touch nothing but dry, dusty soil, and you'll wither.

And then there's actually another layer to idolatry that we need to consider, another type of god that can't be trusted. The idols we've been talking about so far have hardly changed at all over the history of humanity—money, power, sex, status, family, violence, nationalism, or tribalism. But others are idols masquerading as Yahweh. These idols are deeply connected to our current culture, using the conversations of the day to hide themselves in plain sight. These idols take the form of pervasive lies about who God is, lies that twist God's character and deceive us about what God is like. And these are the small-*g* gods that most result in the confusion of *Wait, which god are we talking about, exactly?*

There's "Old Testament god"—who is not actually the God of the Old Testament at all, but instead uses our cultural distance from the Bible to convince us that god cares most about rule-following and rule-breaking, and that god's basic disposition is crotchety.

There's "shame-y god," saying that you kinda suck, but keep trying.

There's "far-off god," who doesn't ever show up or do anything, but holds over you the chance that *maybe this time…*the god will, so you don't dare stop striving.

There's "contractual moralism god," who will protect and provide for you so long as you are basically being good and doing right. In fact, if you are good and do right, that god *owes* you comfort and crisis intervention.

There's "neo-Calvinist reformed god," who is highly concerned about your theological alignment with His (and for sure He's a He); defenders of whom are currently yelling at people who disagree with them on Twitter.

These gods are especially difficult to identify and renounce because they use the Bible to support their existence. The misuse of Scripture aids their persistence, along with the loud, angry loyalty of their followers who are ready to call you a heretic for questioning if that god really is who we should most trust.

But if these gods don't really exist, if they are not what Yahweh is like at all, then they are no different than the idols in the Bible. And, like those idols, when push comes to shove, they will fail to protect and provide for us. They are unworthy answers to the question we talked about earlier, "Whatever happens, it'll all be okay because..."

This matters tremendously when it comes to our kids because whether we are aware of it or not, we are teaching them the end of that sentence. They are learning from us, from our family culture and faith practices or the lack thereof, what answers are possible. They pick up on the alignment or hypocrisy between what we say we trust and what we show we trust. But if idols fail and offer no life, and yet persist all around us, what are we to do? How do we protect ourselves and our kids from being deceived by an idol instead of the true God?

Jesus' disciple Thomas asked a very similar question in John 14: "Lord, we don't know where you are going, so how can we know the way?" (v. 5 NIV). In other words, "How do we know the way that will lead to life? Where are we going? Which God are we following here? You, Jesus, are saying and doing things that are getting mighty close to claiming God's authority. Which means either you are it: Messiah, rescuer, Lord; or you are a dangerous person for us to be associated with the more Rome hears about you."

Jesus answers him, "I am the way and the truth and the life. No one comes to the Father except through me. If you really know me, you will know my Father as well. From now on, you do know him and have seen him" (John 14:6–7 NIV).

Then Philip says to Jesus, "Lord, show us the Father, and we will be satisfied" (John 14: 8 NLT).

Jesus says to him, "Have I been with you all this time, Philip, and yet you still don't know who I am? Anyone who has seen me has seen the Father! So why are you asking me to show [the Father] to you? Don't you believe that I am in the Father and the Father is in me? The words I speak are not my own, but my Father who lives in me does his work through me" (John 14:9–10 NLT).

Earlier I talked about the claims in the Old Testament that Yahweh is the one to trust. When it comes to the New Testament, the claim that keeps popping up throughout is that Jesus is Lord. He's not just a good guy, a wise man, a model of selflessness and how we ought to live. Jesus is Lord. In other words, Jesus *is* Yahweh, walking around in a human body. As Jesus puts it here, Jesus and the Father are one, and anyone who has seen Jesus has seen Yahweh. It is therefore Jesus whom we trust. Whatever happens, it'll be okay because of who Jesus is.

These verses from John are not saying, "Believe in Jesus instead of not believing in Jesus."[9] They are saying that if we want to know

---

[9] They also are certainly not saying, "Believe in Jesus instead of Yahweh," as if Jesus is the kind corrective to the mean "Old Testament god." Incidentally, I once had someone say they *almost* liked something I wrote, except I said Yahweh instead of Jesus, so it made it "too Jewish." With respect to the Jewish tradition (which of course sees this quite differently), Yahweh God of Israel and Jesus Christ of Nazareth are one. The claims about the identity and character of each person of the Trinity are true of the other two members of the Trinity as well.

the way, if we want to know who God is, look at who Jesus is and we'll know.

So, which God are we talking about, exactly? The God who is Jesus. If we want to follow, and want our kids to be anchored to, the true God and not any of the false gods on offer—whether money or shame-y—then our aim should be to help them experience in practical ways a life where whatever happens, it will all be okay because Jesus is Lord.

Whatever we do when it comes to faith should be in order to help them not just intellectually understand that idea and give basic assent to that principle, but also have tangible experiences of that reality. Jesus is Lord.

The whole of the Gospels, of course, give us insight into who Jesus is, and what His Lordship looks like, but maybe one of the most important stories is just two chapters back from Jesus' conversation with Thomas and Philip, in John 12, and if I were telling it to kids, I'd say this:

> Jesus and his followers were heading to Jerusalem, the capital city and home of the temple, so they could celebrate Passover. Passover was the meal remembering how God freed the people from slavery and cared for them on the whole journey to their land, their home. Even though now the people did live in the land, in many ways it didn't feel like home. The reason for that was simple: Rome was in charge. King Caesar was cruel and power-hungry, and his officials and soldiers ensured that the people of Jerusalem, and of everywhere else in Israel, felt keenly aware that their land was not, truly, their own.

Israel longed for a new king who would rescue them. Israel had had many kings over the years. Some were good kings and many were not. (What made a good king was a combination of trying to be a good leader and also trusting just God and no one else.) Did you know God never wanted a king for them? God wanted to be their king, and they could live together in a way that matched who God is. If they did this together, they wouldn't work like any other nation in the area, not by a long shot.

Well, one Sunday in Jerusalem, a new king came to town. He appeared to be just a human king, but because he was Jesus, God in a body, he was so much more. The people in Jerusalem came to the road to see Jesus. They waved palm branches and shouted, "Hosanna!" which means "God saves." They were right: God does, and was, saving.

Jesus rode through the streets on the back of a donkey that day.

The Bible tells us that Jesus' disciples didn't understand what was going on at the time. It was like a puzzle with many pieces, and only after Jesus had died and risen to life again could they click them together. The first piece was from an old prophecy in the Old Testament book of Zechariah that mentioned a king riding on a donkey, just like Jesus was doing. The prophecy was about God's kingdom, how it would be full of peace and would stretch from sea to sea. Did this mean the kingdom was here? Then there was a piece about Jesus acting like he was king, but they knew that Caesar was also king—there's usually just one, after all. So was Jesus actually king and Caesar wasn't?

There was another piece about Jesus' ride: a donkey is a royal ride, but only after winning a war. Did this mean Jesus had already won?

The answer to all three questions is, absolutely, yes.

There is so much that could be said about the story of the triumphal entry to Jerusalem, but we're going to focus on what it tells about who Jesus is, and therefore who God is, before turning to how we can anchor to the reality of Jesus as Lord.

JESUS IS KING

One piece of symbolism we might easily miss these thousands of years later is the significance of Jesus' chosen ride. In addition to being a fulfillment and reference to Zechariah 9:9, where the king comes riding on a donkey, the New Testament scholar Dr. Marianne Meye Thompson points out that in a culture in which most everyone walked, a donkey or mule was actually a royal ride. The crowds, likewise, speak this reality as well, welcoming the king who comes in the name of Yahweh. They understand the symbolism. Jesus is the King of Israel. Caesar may be king of Rome, but that speaks only to the moment, not the ultimate.

JESUS HAS WON

A king riding on a donkey is a king who has already won. A king still at war would be riding on a warhorse. Jesus' victory is already won, meaning we can trust that God is truly King. The victory is not uncertain or precarious, which means now is the time for peace. God is the sort of king who relies neither on violence nor force to get God's way, but rather one whose very presence brings peace.

JESUS' VICTORY IS BROUGHT THROUGH SACRIFICE

The people likely expected a show of power by which Jesus would defeat the Roman legions and drive them out of Jerusalem.[10] If Rome operates on violence for compliance, force and power as the norm, surely one greater than Rome would use those tools, too, just...more. Right? That's what it means to be powerful? That's what it means to be the true king?

But John tells us the story of a very different show of power, one that begins with death on a cross, and then the defeat of death itself through the resurrection. Jesus is King, yes, but a king who sacrifices himself for his people, whose victory is won not through violence, but humility.

JESUS BRINGS LIFE, EVEN OUT OF DEATH

Jesus is a king who brings life. The story of the triumphal entry in John is set right after Jesus raises Lazarus from the dead, and John refers to that sign as he tells this story as well. The people who come out to welcome Jesus to Jerusalem have heard about what Jesus did

---

[10] This is often called *messianic expectation*.

in raising Lazarus from the dead. John includes this reference intentionally to help us see further what type of king Jesus is: a king who brings life out of death for his people.

JESUS' KINGDOM IS EVERYWHERE, FOR EVERYONE

Jesus' kingdom will mean life not just for Israel but for the whole world. The Zechariah passage that's coming to life before the people's eyes in the triumphal entry to Jerusalem includes within it an expectation of what else will be true when the king comes: It will be a sign of peace, and a worldwide kingdom, all under the rule of Yahweh. The kingdom will be from sea to sea, including all the nations. Yahweh is a God of peace, who cares about the whole earth.

Add it all up, and the triumphal entry paints a picture of Jesus, the victorious King, whose victory is won not through violence but through sacrifice, and who is committed to bringing life to the whole earth. That's who Jesus is. That's who our God is. That's who we can trust.

Both the gods of the ancient world and the contemporary gods that complete the "whatever happens" sentence have one major thing in common: They fail us. They don't come through.

But they lure us all, playing on our fears that maybe what we have been trusting isn't going to be enough. And yet, our fears can be helpful, because they both point out those idols that tempt us with their promises, *and* expose the truth that those promises are ultimately empty, that the idols are not worthy of our trust.

For my husband, who won't mind me telling on him a bit, the thing that most terrifies him is mental decline, Alzheimer's, dementia. He's not looking forward to bodily aging or death, but those don't scare him like his mind breaking down. Why? Because one of his temptations is to put his trust in the idol of intelligence, and the thought of losing his mental acuity exposes the reality that at some point that intelligence will disappear. And when that happens, his trust in being able to think and talk his way through a problem (a great skill of his) will be in vain. Other people have creeping anxiety around the state of the economy and the stock market, because if those drop, it will expose the lie that the money they have invested will keep them safe. Others are terrified that something will happen to their family, their kids, not simply because they love their kids, which is of course a good thing, but terrified beyond that because losing their kids would expose the lie that it'll be okay because they've got their family. It's not just evil things that can be idols, remember. The prophet Jeremiah accuses Israel of making an idol out of Yahweh's temple itself, in fact. Family, work, church, they're all good things; they can also all become idols when we rely on them for our security instead of on God.

SPIRAL THE ATTRIBUTE

In addition to the story of the triumphal entry, here are some ideas for spiraling back to Jesus as Lord in other parts of the Bible:

- Look for Old Testament echoes. For example, right after the exodus the people receive the law and God says, "I'm Yahweh your God, who brought you out of Egypt, you'll have no other gods besides me" (see

> Exod. 20:2–3). The people are being reminded who they should trust: Yahweh God is Lord, not only of the people, but of the world.
>
> - Saul meets Jesus. One of the things that angers Saul about these new Jesus followers is how they claim Jesus is Lord. And yet, after meeting Jesus personally, this becomes his main message as well: The risen Jesus is Lord, and that changes everything.

In order to move forward with our kids and faith, we have to face the fears that have lured us toward idols.

Fear has cast a shadow over children's faith formation. Our fear has made an idol out of obedience. Perhaps that's the fear of our family falling apart, the fear of going through overwhelming grief or hardship, the fear of the consequence of a choice that can't be taken back. We fear an uncontrollable, unknowable, and uncertain world.

Fear lures us until it has a death grip on every detail of our lives and our kids' lives as we try desperately to make sure those things don't happen. We are desperate for something or someone we can turn to so that bad things won't happen. Most idols promise us not just protection and provision, but *prevention*.

Fear moves obedience from its proper place as a secondary response that comes naturally out of trust to being an idol of its own. Whatever happens, it'll all be okay if we are obedient. If our kids are obedient. We can obey our way into God's favor, good-choice ourselves out of pain. And sure, that's a little self-righteous, but what's the alternative?

The alternative is to trust Yahweh, not idols. The alternative is to declare Jesus is Lord, and let that shape your life.

I warn you, though, trusting in Jesus is not a prevention strategy that makes sure what we fear won't happen. Those fears may indeed be realized, and yet they won't consume us. As God has proved time and again in the stories of Scripture and in the lives of those who have put their trust in Jesus through the years, even when the worst happens, it will be okay, somehow, because of who God is. The God who is good, powerful, just, joyful, and with us is really and truly Lord.

Jesus is Lord.

My kids' grades. Their friend circles. Their college prospects. Their character.

Are not.

Are those things both valuable and important? Absolutely. Can you trust them to keep you safe? You cannot. And whatever happens, it will all be okay because of who God is, not what your kids do.

With this as our anchor, let's turn to some habits and practices that can specifically shape our families around Jesus' lordship.

WHAT ISN'T LORD

One way to help kids relate to their activities and their possessions is to talk about how those things are good, but they aren't what matters most. Have conversations about the things people put their trust in: being the best at sports, always getting good grades, being popular, having the newest shoes or gaming system. (As kids get older, you can also categorize these examples to connect them to the ways adults do this too: status, opportunity, talent, hard work, etc.) You might say, "People get to choose who or what they trust to take care of them. A lot of people trust themselves most. As a family, we practice trusting just God. The things we have or are good at are really good, and we're grateful for them. But they aren't what we trust."

CELEBRATING CHRISTMAS AND EASTER

The Christian tradition unites around two major holidays: Christmas to celebrate the incarnation—God becoming human in Jesus; and Easter to celebrate the resurrection. Both of these holidays:

- Offer an incredible opportunity for clarifying what matters most to our families. Since each is not just a day, but a season, there's more time for faith-forming practices.
- Have fun traditions that cultivate family bonds.
- Include opportunities to connect with justice-oriented organizations for their seasonal efforts.
- Have a series of key stories from Scripture that you can explore together, looking for who God is and what God's like.
- Repeat year after year, allowing you to focus on individual concepts in simple terms, because this Christmas or Easter is not your only opportunity to get your kids to understand the biblical story or its related theology. Everything can grow deeper, richer, and more complex over time.

In other words, these two holiday seasons offer space for every principle that we've talked about to be put into practice. Celebrating them with intention, attending to the threads they weave, can go a long way in nurturing your child's faith as they offer the chance to explore what *Jesus is Lord* meant then and what it can mean for them now.

At the same time, both of these holidays are often observed in ways that undercut that very message. Instead of Jesus being Lord, a host of other things become lord of the holiday season. We worship family as lord. Consumerism is lord. Holiday magic and memory-making are lord. Tradition is lord. Our bank statements and calendar apps for December and March or April can tell us a lot about who or what is being worshipped each season.

Please hear me: There is no need to eliminate family time, presents, or decorations. (Unless you *want* to stop attending Aunt Nina's seven-hour sing-along, in which case you can tell her I said it was bad for your child's faith and I'll gladly accept her angry DM.) There's no need to ax the egg hunt or become a grinch for Jesus. What's crucial is to (1) be cautious of ways you actually negate what you claim the holiday is about by the way it gets celebrated; and (2) decide how you will hold on to Jesus as Lord in a way your child can participate in and thereby retain as they grow.

BIBLICAL EXPLORATION

God-Centered Storytelling

When it comes to the Christmas story, Mary's worthiness and trust, Joseph's obedience, the shepherds being selected, the wise men's worship—all of these are secondary to what God is doing by becoming a person like us, the one who will be faithful to Israel's story thus far, and who will clarify where God is going in the future. Putting God at the center of the Christmas stories allows new layers of meaning to emerge. Mary can be both trusting and afraid, like us; Joseph can be both upset and obedient, like us; the shepherds can be both ordinary and specially selected, like us; the wise men can be both pagan astrologists and rightly worshipful (and, well, you may or may not be one for astrology, but we all do trust God and something else sometimes, even as we want to trust God alone).

Likewise, at Easter the crowd's streetside worship, Peter's denial, Judas's betrayal, the women's testimony, all find their meaning in relation to what Jesus is doing to be faithful and obedient to his mission to inaugurate the reign of God on earth and what God is doing in raising Jesus to life again. Every person who encounters Jesus through the Easter story helps us see more clearly the purposes of God. We don't need the people to be any better than they are, because it is God's work and power that we're hoping to trust.

Do Less on Purpose

Divide the holiday stories into many smaller stories and talk about them before and after the holiday proper. This allows different elements of God's action to be more easily identified (and keeps it shorter). For Christmas, that could be: angel visits Mary, angel visits Joseph, Jesus is born, shepherds visit Jesus, wise men visit Jesus. For Easter, this can be: triumphal entry, Jesus washes the disciples' feet, the rest of the Last Supper, Jesus dies on the cross, the women discover the empty tomb, the road to Emmaus, Jesus makes breakfast on the beach.

Explore and Respond

In addition to listening to or reading the stories, you could draw one as a comic strip, play songs that tell the story (and perhaps even compare the lyrics to the biblical narrative), make one a Mad Lib, or play with nativity pieces. Both stories are especially ripe with the opportunities to wonder, express surprise, and share what is both wonderful and wild about these narratives.

One tool I've used for these stories is a "weird-o-meter," a hand-drawn and decorated thermometer that measures the weirdness in a story. As I tell it, I pause on purpose along the way to ask: *How weird does this part seem to you?* and kids rate that plot point. There is no right or wrong measurement, but the weird-o-meter creates space for awe at what God has done and doubt about how extraordinary it is. We want to welcome both awe and doubt from kids, if they feel them, and a whimsical tool can be a useful one.

Experiences, Rituals, and Traditions

From treats for neighbors to playlists, from special foods to service projects, opportunities abound for experiences and traditions that connect these holidays to who God is. As we feast, we experience God's abundance. As we gather, we experience being part of the family of God. As we receive gifts, we experience unearned goodness.

When I ask my own children about the ways we celebrate holidays, one favorite that tops their lists, for Christmas and Easter, is our Story Scavenger Hunt. I divide up the pieces of the biblical story, and then also create clues to lead the way through, ending up at either their Christmas stockings or their Easter baskets. While our version happens to be *very* involved and takes an hour (there are lockboxes, UV pens, white-crayon messages on white paper that you paint to reveal, maps...it's a whole thing), a similar, scaled-down version could be a fun way to weave together several values at once.

YOU ASK

What do we do about Santa?

I know better than to answer this, except to say: If you don't do Santa, you can still include Santa through, as Fred Rogers reminds us, "the land of make-believe." Santa can be imaginary, and imaginary is fun. If you do choose to include Santa, the key is to give thought to how that ends when the time comes. You need to end Santa in a way that helps your kid navigate that one invisible man, Santa, is not real, but another invisible man, Jesus, is. So think about what you'd like to say to your kid about Santa, knowing that's the deeper issue to be sensitive about.

Relationships

Both Christmas and Easter are often celebrated with others. In the US, that typically takes the form of church attendance for an hour followed by time with family. The question to ask of that form, or whatever form your holiday observance takes, is: How does this help your child connect with the larger community of faith, especially the people who are supporting them in their faith journey? Sometimes the pace of the holidays crowds out the chance for genuine relational connection. While this is understandable, perhaps the threads your child most needs are not woven through activities, but through conversation or shared meals, the chance to be asked about their life by an adult who has nowhere to be but with them, listening.

Christmas and Easter can be especially robust faith experiences for our kids, but they aren't automatically so. They are equally likely to be frenzied, consumeristic, and pressured, like the culture tells us they inevitably have to be. So you must weave your own web, crafting an approach to Christmas and Easter that is joyful and sustainable, one that is life-giving for your family (and, to be clear, that includes you, not everyone *but* you, as you act like a holiday fairy exhausting yourself to make the magic). That could mean creating traditions that you stick to so you don't have to re-create your plan every year (this is why our scavenger hunts are only slightly different from year to year). That could mean doing less, so there's more margin for everyone all season long.

NAVIGATING THE BELIEFS OF OTHERS

As a child, I had a good friend whose family faith culture was more conservatively inclined than my own. One way that played out was that she seemed a bit afraid of those who were not Christians. Her family spent time "preparing" for hypothetical conversations where these kids would "challenge" her faith with their own. This left her with a caricatured version of most other major religions, because her understanding was formed around apologetics designed to confront them.

The tension for those who declare Jesus is Lord is that it's a solo role. Nothing and no one else is Lord. The singularity of the claim is enough to ensure that your kids will cross paths with peers whose families hold different worldviews than your own. While I'm sure my friend's family did what seemed best, I would venture to suggest that mounting a defense need not be the core focus when coaching your child for these conversations. Instead, here are four elements you can include in ongoing conversation about differing worldviews:

- **Image-bearing respect.** When you speak about others' beliefs, even if you disagree wildly or have a deeply emotional reaction to them, be sure your tone is calm and respectful. Doing so models this truth: No one loses the image of God within them by believing the wrong things, and we practice honoring that, even as we see things very differently.

- **Simple accuracy.** Imagine the tables were turned, and an adult was explaining your own views to your child's peer. That peer then does what most kids do, and tells your child what the adult said. What would you want them to say about you? Your own words about others' beliefs should be simple and fair, such that the other person would say, "Yeah, that's the gist of what I believe."

- **What _I_ believe, not what _we_ believe.** Describe the ways you disagree, the differences in theological understanding, or the distinctions between another worldview and your own as just that: your own. Adults sometimes say to kids, "This person or group believes X, but _we_ believe Y." However, your child is growing into what they believe. What's more, your child's love for you can make them feel pressured to align with you, and shut down the curious conversation that actually helps them determine their own views. Instead you can say, "I believe Y is true because…and I'm so glad you asked about this, because I'm here to help you figure out if Y is true too. What other questions do you have right now?"

- **Important history.** Has this tradition or group been the subject of discrimination or violence historically, especially at the hands of politically or culturally powerful Christians? Share this information with them, so they understand why care and respect are so critical. This might sound like, "We always want to treat people kindly, of course. But it's also important that you know that [group] has been treated especially poorly in the past. Sometimes when people feel sure they are right, they think that makes it okay to be mean to folks they're 'sure' are wrong. This has been especially true when a group feels sure they are right *and* they have a lot of power. But even when we hold very different views, it's important that everyone be safe, and for us to be part of not just kindness, but protection for all people."

Despite the wide difference between our time and place and the world of the Bible, the question remains: *Which gods do you worship, and what are they like?* The answer to the question is shown through who and what we trust. It is undeniably challenging to trust Jesus, just Jesus, perhaps most of all because that means turning away from more tangible options, ones where we wield more control or at least maintain the illusion of doing so. More challenging still is helping your child have eyes to see how it can be true that this Jesus is King, and has won, and is bringing life. It doesn't seem to be true so much of the time. This is where we find kinship with the people in the world of the Bible, both in the Old and the New Testaments. It often did not seem to be that God was reigning and the world would be right. So they lamented and raged, wondered and wept. All this, and more, was met by God with tenderness, and still is, because Jesus our Lord is infinitely tender to the reality of being human.

CHAPTER 11

Where Webs Begin

As we draw near the end of this book, it's time to bring it all together, taking all we've discussed thus far and homing in on how, in your life, with your child, this will take shape. I'm not going to tell you what to do (and you're not surprised by now), because your web is your own. Instead, I want to walk you through a four-part process that will help you get started now, applying all we've talked about to your family's unique web of faith. This process is also what you'll return to anytime your family's faith culture is needing some new practices, or your family has entered a new season together, or what you've been doing just isn't working anymore.

How do you start spinning your family's web of faith? Name. Narrow. Try. Tinker.

NAME

Begin by naming two important things. First, **name the season you're in.** What is simply true of your day-to-day life right now? Are there activities happening? What's work like? When does sleep happen?

For example, if it was August in my family, I'd be thinking of how soccer has begun, school will start at the end of the month, and my kids (still) wake up before 6:00 a.m. All of those are part of our season.

Second, **name your options.** This is a brain dump and you could do it several ways; there isn't a right or wrong approach. For instance:

- Take the ideas that have resonated with you or that you've generated yourself as you've read this book and bring them all together in one list.
- Personalize the list of God's attributes that you'd most like to focus upon as anchors. They may come from the previous chapters, or you could add in ones that are personally significant for you or your child. After naming those attributes, parallel the process from part 2: What Bible stories highlight the attribute that you could

explore? What experiences, traditions, or rituals might help your kid anchor to it?

- Ideate by the type of faith practices.

Bible exploration	Car conversation
	Bedtime stories
	Bible memory verses
	Holiday stories (for Christmas and Easter)
Sabbath	Family Day
	Sunday dinner
	Game night
	Vacation
Rites of passage	Baptism
	Communion
	Grade transitions
Prayer	Draw
	Finish the sentence
	Move and pray
	Labyrinth
Community-building	Have people for dinner
	Park meetups
	Participating in a faith community
Service and justice	Compost
	Giving
	Learning about injustice
Identity-shaping	Birthdays
	Life-giving mantras
	Making (art, music, dance)
	Holiday traditions

- Use the flow of the day as your jumping-off point:
    - Mornings: How do we start our day connected to God?
    - Car time: What makes space for questions and conversations as we drive?
    - Off to school or play: What words send my child out into the world?
    - Welcoming home: How do we transition to home or into our evening?
    - Meals: Are there meal traditions that can support our faith?
    - Bedtime: How do we close our day connected to God?

- Name values you hold as a family of faith, then identify the practices that embody those values.

Grace	A template for how we apologize A mantra to remind us that mistakes do not define us
Wonder	Get out in nature Imaginative storytelling to enter Bible stories
Neighborhood	Become a regular in certain shops or restaurants Walk and pray for our neighbors
Gratitude	Keep a jar to notice goodness Category prayers (Thanks, God, for [people], [places], [meeting needs], etc.)
Justice	Write officials Attend a community action event

NARROW

Once you've come up with a variety of options, it's time for step two: Narrow to just a few practices. The first criteria for narrowing is **anchors**. How does this practice help you, your child, and your family collectively anchor to who God is?

You might ask:

- Why are we doing this practice?
- What do I hope this practice forms in us over time?
- Do I feel clear about the connection between this idea and one or more aspects of God's character? If not, could I adjust the practice to strengthen that connection?

The next criteria is **fit**. How does this practice fit with your real family? You might ask yourself, and talk with your partner about:

- Does this idea fit who we are—our family's personality, culture, and overall vibe?
- Does it fit this season of our life together, or would it possibly be better in another season?
- Does this practice stretch us, but in a good way?
- Are we doing this because I think we "should"?
- Do my kids seem to enjoy or resist this practice?

The key is to move from the long list of options to just two or three things to start with. There is always time to add more later on, but too much at once will be overwhelming. You're creating a sustainable rhythm, not doing *Extreme Home Makeover: Faith Edition*.

TRY

After you narrow, it's time to try them out. Begin by picking a time to try them. As you think about time, consider **frequency, time of day**, and **duration**.

- Frequency: Does this practice make the most sense if it happens daily, weekly, monthly, or even annually?
- Is it okay for this practice to happen when we feel like it? Or should it be a commitment we stick to?
- Time of day: When do we all (kids and adults alike) have the best energy for this particular practice? For instance, your kids may have a bedtime energy that just doesn't match the beautiful, calm worship playlist you'd like to have on.
- Duration: Do we have any practices we find helpful, but we need to adjust how often we do them or how long they last?

TINKER

Fourth, after you've tried, it's time to tinker. Treat this like an experiment. As Emily P. Freeman says, "Pick what you like; see how it grows." After trying something for a while, circle back and ask yourself questions like: What worked well? What did not? Should we adjust the practice or push pause on it for now?

As you evaluate your experiments, it can also be helpful to interpret the challenges you experience. There are a lot of things that threaten to ruin our rhythm, but if we can identify them, we can also tinker accordingly. You can do this with the practices you already have in place as well to see which ones should stay, which ones should be tinkered with, and which ones should, perhaps, be cycled out.

In my experience there are six major disrupters that throw people off groove when they are trying to put faith practices into a joyful, sustainable rhythm of life.

Pace	The practices you're trying don't fit into the speed of your life. If you try to put them on the calendar, you know they'll just get pushed out again by another activity.	Do we need to change our pace or our practices so they fit into our calendar more easily?
Personality	The practices you're trying may be great for someone else, but they don't fit your family's collective personality.	Are we trying practices that we will basically enjoy? If not, what could we experiment with instead?
Preparation	Whenever you think about incorporating a faith practice, it's hard to start because you aren't ready ahead of time to make it as successful as possible. This derails both experimenting with new practices and sustaining the ones that work.	What needs to happen before we do this together so it can go as well as possible?

Protecting time	You know what you'd like to do but need to protect the time to do it. You find that your rhythm lacks consistency because other things tend to fill in when you'd hoped to do something faith-oriented.	When can I schedule this practice so it won't get bumped by something else, even something good?
Connected to the person	Things you are trying feel religious, but you aren't sure your family sees how they connect to the person of Jesus. The challenge is not necessarily what to do or when, but being sure everyone knows why.	Am I clear on what attributes of God this helps us uncover or connect to? Have I shared that with everyone?
Perfectionistic	When it's time to engage in a faith practice, you expect it to go a particular way that feels right, then struggle to adjust if people won't cooperate. The time can become overfocused on how it happens so that it's perfect.	What can I release as an expectation so that we can really engage as ourselves?

To illustrate how this process might play out, here's a recent example from my own family.

I mentioned before that we have a Family Day for regular rest and play, and that we'd added Sunday dinner to our Sabbath rhythm. Sunday dinner came about through this very processs. We named our season: Our kids were returning to in-person school after the time of at-home school necessitated by COVID. Our pace was changing as some activities, like soccer on Saturdays, became available again.

We named our options, starting with what we hoped our kids might experience of God. As I mentioned before, we were captivated by the biblical story of tithe, which I unpacked in chapter 8, and I wondered if it could lead us forward. I narrowed our ideas to things that would be enjoyable for our kids (as opposed to a stretching practice, like generosity with their own money).

With a sense of clarity about how this practice could connect to the person of Yahweh God, we realized we were not just willing, but wanting to change our pace on Sunday afternoons, to slow down sooner and ease out of our weekend. It became easier to protect the time once our kids understood what we were doing together, and enjoyed that they were a big part of deciding which restaurant we'd order from each week.

But before that happened, trying out Sunday dinner sucked. Without knowing our options for dinner, we clumsily tried to pick a place we could all agree on, getting hangrier by the minute. Our first week we agreed on our favorite taqueria, only to drive up and realize they had changed their hours and were closed on Sundays. There were tears; I won't say whose. But we approached this as an experiment, which helped us tinker until it began to work. For instance, we made a list of local, family-owned restaurants that were open on Sundays and that all of us enjoyed eating at. Now, Sunday dinner is a vibrant part of our family faith rhythm. It has yielded a lot of great faith conversations with our kids, who are not of the personality to talk about God or the Bible on demand, meaning we have to create space and stay on our toes.

Name. Narrow. Try. Tinker.

Anytime your family feels stuck, or your kid moves into a new season, or new faith questions crop up, you can return again to this process: Name your season and your option, narrow to just a couple of practice ideas, try something, and tinker with it. As your kids get older, they can be more involved in deciding how this looks and what you do together, as well as beginning to consider these same steps for themselves.

When I say that your family needs to weave your own web, this is how you get there. It's intentional and ordinary. It's spiritual and also simple. Such is the power of weaving your own web. You get to partner with the Holy Spirit to craft a way of living life that is joyful, sustainable, and anchored to the character of God. Instead of trying to shove your family into a box, you let your web take on the unique shape and structure it needs to help you all know and trust God more and more. All the while, it feels like you, the way that weaving is ordinary for the spider. And ordinary is enough.

You'll know it's working when your child begins to ask you more questions. I know—at times you wonder if more questions are even possible. These questions will be about God and the Bible, and also why the world works the way it does, why people seem to be the way they are. They are questions that invite you to tell the story of God. You'll know it's working when your family experiences more of the life Jesus offered: joyful and justice-seeking, kind and compassionate, connected and able to mend disconnection. You'll know it's working when you find, sometimes, your child takes a next right step in their faith, and talks about God in increasingly personal ways, like a person they really know. Perhaps best of all, you'll know it's working in ways I can only guess at, but as the one who knows your child best, you'll see it. There'll be ways that are just…them, coming alive to the love of God.

SOME FINAL THOUGHTS

You likely know by now, but when it comes to faith and our kids, there are no guarantees, magic bullets, or surefire formulas. Believe me, researchers have tried to find it. But perhaps God doesn't want us to follow a formula. Perhaps God dreams of families weaving webs all their own, each one uniquely adapted to the people who share it. You cannot be sure how your child's faith will turn out. You can raise them in a way that feels honoring to God and to your kid, a way that you'll feel deeply proud of, even if life takes you and them to unexpected places. You can follow Jesus, and invite them in, in meaningful and intentional ways.

It feels terribly risky. How do we know we can afford to go slow, weaving strand by strand, allowing a child's faith to take its own shape? Our answer is the same as the one we point them to: because of who God is.

The God who creates an abundantly good world, one that's sure to expand in the most diverse ways possible to become full of goodness and beauty. The God who is relentless in keeping commitments, unending in showing faithfulness. The God who became a person like us, because human partnership is the plan when it comes to redeeming the world. The God who partners with you as you help this child grow into just who they were made to be, never leaving you alone. The God who can be trusted.

Operating out of a trust-based paradigm isn't just for your child. It's for you, offering you the courage to choose a woven faith and trust that it's not tatters and tangles, but strong and beautiful.

I am often asked if there is any way to raise kids in a faith that they won't need to deconstruct.

It depends on what you mean by that. There is a way to raise your kids in a faith that does not hurt them. A faith that isn't a wound. The way you follow Jesus together can be full of grace and kindness, joy and generosity, apologies and mending. You can nurture a faith your kid doesn't have to heal from.

There is, however, no avoiding a season of reexamination, of questions and searching. Call it deconstruction, perhaps, though I find it helpful to remember that this experience is not novel, and has gone by many names, from the hopeful, like when students in a research group described how much bigger God was seeming to them as they moved into adulthood, to the painful, like the "dark night of the soul."

One such name for the time of reexamining is moratorium, from the work of psychologist James Marcia. Marcia describes a progression from what he calls *foreclosure* (a rigid sense of identity that is inherited and has not been explored or experimented with) to *moratorium* (a time when identity, including religious identity, is questioned and opened up to change). Moratorium can appear on the surface to be a "walking back" from what a young person used to "believe," but in the bigger picture of identity development, it's a normal, healthy, and expected season, one that leads to a person truly owning for themselves various aspects of their identity. As it relates to faith development, moratorium is a needed time of reexamination, when a person takes the faith they inherited and sorts out what pieces of it stay with them for adulthood, what pieces are released, and what new things they might want to learn or consider more deeply.

Moratorium is not the same as deconstruction (notably Marcia's work is from 1980, long before deconstruction became a Thing on the internet), but they are close enough to one another to motivate my response to this desire for an un-deconstructable faith. If we do it right, our kids will, at some point, enter moratorium, because we will not allow any fear about their possible changing faith to force them to remain in foreclosure. If we do it right, moratorium will be expected, and supported. It might still be scary, but more in the way an adventure into the unknown is scary, yet welcome.

I have an unproven theory that many of my generation were denied their own moratorium. Whether motivated by fear, control, or something else, they were not welcomed into the season of revisiting inherited faith, let alone supported through it. That in itself is a wound, though I imagine the adults who inflicted it would say that they were simply focusing on passing on a resilient faith. Not having the chance to experience moratorium as an emerging adult would very likely bring someone to that phase later on, because it still matters. Hence a number of people in my generation of "church kids" find themselves revisiting their faith, taking stock of broken strands, and trying to discern if they are anchored to who God is or to something else. This examination has the potential to make our faith far more resilient.

Resilience in faith circles is often misrepresented as something firm and immovable, built brick by brick, each doctrine defined, each principle provided, each application prescribed. Resilience, according to the spider, is drawn out of the ability to flex in order to withstand stress, to bend in significant ways without breaking. It is also the ability to reweave the broken strands, so as not to lose your home, and to do so without becoming too exhausted to go on.

Woven faith is resilient faith.

Woven faith, anchored to who God is, and yet uniquely shaped, has the strength to withstand real life. When the internal strands are pliable, change and challenges don't destroy. To be sure, the process of revisiting, questioning, and at times reimagining how those strands connect is stressful. But it's the stress of strength. And yes, inevitably, some strands will break, beliefs we used to hold and don't anymore. The breaking of a strand is a loss, to be sure. We grieve it, but it doesn't need to be the end.

I'm done with the hollow promise that if we just use the Bible to raise good kids and point to Jesus as the reason they should behave, then they will be good kids, and they will behave. They might not. But beyond that, I'm done with the hollowness of using the Bible and using Jesus. I want my kids to know Jesus. Really know what he is like so that not only can they hear the invitation, but they also are excited to say yes to joining him in the work of restoring all things.

For far too long we haven't treated children with the care that they deserve. We've rushed them instead of giving them their own time to get to know God.

We've shamed them because we wanted them to behave and comply and that really is about making our lives easier. In that way we have taken God's name in vain, claiming that God is the one who wants them to put away their dishes and tidy their rooms.

We've scared them, because we were scared that maybe God's love and grace aren't actually strong enough to win in the end. We show that we aren't sure God is trustworthy. I'm certain God is tender toward that doubt, but I think God is equally tender toward the child who need not fear. God is magnetic, I'm convinced, and yet we approach children as though we don't think they would actually be drawn to God, given the chance to get to know Them.

But if we didn't shame or scare them and instead just introduced them to God, wouldn't they find their hearts burning within them? Perhaps kids spend childhood on their own Emmaus road, with Jesus right there beside them. Is it possible that we grown-ups are like the story of Scripture, like broken bread, a tool God can use such that a child's eyes will be opened to the Jesus who is with them?

Dear reader, may the Holy Spirit lead you toward the children in your life with tenderness, compassion, and gentleness. May you know that, by God's grace, you can focus not on just right behavior or even just right beliefs, but rather on the living God, and God's grand story of redeeming this whole world.

ACKNOWLEDGMENTS

I have been looking forward to writing this page for months. Because every idea in this book was first experienced with real people, played out in actual life. My deepest gratitude goes to:

My agent, Andrea Heinecke, for your support, guidance, and encouragement. My editor, Beth Adams, who cared as much for my readers as I did, and what a gift that is. Vice President of Hachette Nashville Daisy Hutton, for your vision for a fresh conversation about faith and kids. Laini, Anika, Stacey, Cat, and the wonderful publishing team at Worthy, for bringing books to life in a life-giving way.

Brad Griffin, for allowing me to be a research assistant when I had no clue what that meant, starting me down the rabbit hole of research. Kara Powell and the Fuller Youth Institute team, your work has mattered so much to me and countless others.

Three children's ministry pastors mark my life: Carolyn Hamic, who created the best children's ministry a kid could ever hope to grow up in, and I was one such kid. Sheryl Walden, who first let me serve in our children's ministry at age 16 and mentored me in countless ways over the years to follow. Mindy Stoms, who knew it was time for something new at Willow and invited me to play a part in it.

To the Promiseland Team of Willow Creek South Barrington, if I'm right about anything I wrote here, I owe it to what I saw happen each weekend in our rooms as you all created space for the Holy Spirit to meet kids.

Hillside Community Church, I love Jesus because of how, as a young person, I watched you love him, love one another, and love the world. You were the most fun, and I would not be who I am without you. My gratitude for you is immeasurable. Pomona Valley Church, thank you for letting me be your pastor. It's a questionable call, but then again, what's new?

Curtis, on a practical level, this book is better for your many thoughtful edits. But much more importantly, you have made ministry possible for me over and over again through encouragement and cooking, script doctoring sermons, and solo-parenting while I travel. I love you, and thank you.

Mom and Dad, thank you for finding a way to follow Jesus as the family we were instead of fitting a mold (like we ever could). I love you GABAMTTWWW.

Riley and Peyton, I hope your dad and I help you as you get to know God, but I hope you also know you have helped me know God better too. Riley, you are a gift and joy. Peyton, I love you and I like you a very lot. I'm so glad I'm your mom.

ABOUT THE AUTHOR

Meredith Miller is a pastor and a parent who has spent most of the past twenty years helping families follow Jesus. She has been involved with the Fuller Youth Institute since 2007, and from 2014 to 2019, she was Curriculum Director for the children's ministry at Willow Creek Community Church in Chicago. Meredith holds a Master of Divinity degree from Fuller Theological Seminary, as well as a BA in Religious Studies and Spanish Language & Literature from Westmont College. She is pastor of Pomona Valley Church and calls Southern California home.